Most Common
Mistakes
in English

An English learner's guide

by

Jakub Marian

First Edition, September 2014

ISBN-13: 978-1502304636

Printed by:

On-Demand Publishing LLC, 100 Enterprise Way, Suite A200
Scotts Valley, CA 95066, USA

Author and Publisher:

Jakub Marian, Sewanstraße 217, 10319, Berlin, Germany

Before you start reading

You are reading the paperback version of this book. If you happen to have found this book freely available on the Internet (from an illegal source), please consider buying a legal copy (there is a PDF, Kindle, and Paperback edition) which is also the only one guaranteed to be up to date. You can find links to all the versions at

http://jakubmarian.com/english-mistakes/

You may be also interested in my book about the most common **pronunciation mistakes** in English, which you can find at

http://jakubmarian.com/pronunciation/

If you bought this book, you are allowed to make as many (electronic or physical) copies as you wish and distribute these to all members of your household. You are not allowed to make the book available publicly; if you wish to send it to someone not within your household, simply buy another paper or electronic copy.

If you find any error in the book, please send an email with a description of the error to

errors@jakubmarian.com

Table of Contents

Foreword

Unlike French with its *Académie française* or Russian with the *Russian Language Institute*, English has no central regulatory body. There is no single "standard English". "Standard" English grammar, spelling, and pronunciation are governed by influential dictionaries, grammar books, style guides, and by recommended standards used in schools in various English-speaking countries.

Nevertheless, there are many rules you should follow if you want to sound natural; for example, if you say "he taked" instead of "he took", you are guaranteed to be perceived as not using proper English by virtually all native speakers. In this book, we shall explore common mistakes English learners make which break such essential rules, i.e. which truly make you sound non-native or which can cause misunderstanding.

Since the whole book is written in English, I assume the reader is already an intermediate or advanced English learner (otherwise he or she wouldn't be able to read it), and the mistakes mentioned in the book were selected accordingly.

I believe any intermediate or advanced English learner can profit from reading this book. Of course, it is impossible to include *all mistakes* English learners make in a single book, but if you know the basics and learn all the topics presented in this book, you should be able to express yourself (in terms of grammar and syntax) like a native speaker most of the time.

It should be also noted that American and British English are given a completely equal treatment, and whenever there are important differences between the two variants, the book explains them appropriately.

Introduction

Before we move on to the mistakes, there's one important thing you should realize: Each language is different, and what may be readily expressible in your mother tongue may be hard to express in English and vice versa. When you read about the mistakes, do not try to understand the English construction through translation into your mother tongue. If you make a mistake subconsciously, the corresponding construction in your mother tongue probably doesn't agree with the English one, and trying to understand it using translation may only confuse you further.

You should develop an intuition for what sounds natural, and what does not. For example, as we will see later in the book, we never use the present perfect with a specific time in the past (e.g. "I have done it yesterday"), which may be surprising because such usage would be correct in most European languages. You should just try to remember that "I have done it yesterday" does not sound natural in English, while "I did it yesterday" does, without any need for translation.

A little note about the order of the mistakes in the book: Topics are divided into five categories, which could be summarized as *things, verbs, adjectives, prepositions,* and *commas*. Within each category, topics are ordered so that the whole book is logically coherent; if one topic follows logically after another, it comes after it in the book as well.

However, apart from that, the ordering doesn't follow any particular scheme. I tried to make the topics varied enough to make reading of the book enjoyable (without having to read about similar topics over and over again). If you need to find a particular topic, you should be able to do so using the table of contents at the beginning of the book.

Mistakes with articles, nouns, and pronouns

NOUNS WITH IDENTICAL SINGULAR AND PLURAL FORMS

When we mention irregular plural forms in English, "children", "men", and "women" are three examples that spring to mind, but there are many more nouns whose plural is not formed by adding -s or -es. Among these, some of the most perplexing are those that do not change at all to form the plural.

Let's go through some of the most important ones (a few more will be treated later when we speak about nouns that end in -s in their singular form), always with an example sentence to help you remember the correct form:

- **aircraft, hovercraft, spacecraft**, and other "-craft" vehicles
  There are two aircraft prepared for landing.

- **bison**: *The bison were grazing in the distance.*

- **cod**: *The cod are known to migrate in large numbers.*

- **deer**: *Deer are an easy prey for wolves.*

- **fish**: *Three fish swim in the fish tank.*

- **moose**: *Moose actually belong to the deer family.*

- **offspring**: *The fox gave birth to five offspring.*

- **pike**: *The pike are big freshwater predatory fish.*

- **salmon**: *Salmon are often seen jumping over dangerous waterfalls.*

- **sheep**: *One sheep, two sheep, three sheep...*

- **shrimp**: *Shrimp are among the most commonly eaten animals.*

- **trout**: *The trout are fish related to the salmon.*

Note that many species of fish were left out from the list. Referring to fish using the same singular and plural form is extremely common, but actual usage varies somewhat among different regions, so it is advisable to consult a dictionary when writing about a particular species.

Also note that the names of animals mentioned above are sometimes used in the plural to refer to several species bearing the same name, for example:

> *The diversity of the reef's fishes [fish species] is threatened by human activity.*

Furthermore, there are a few nouns that can take either regular or irregular plural forms:

- **boar**: *He saw several boar(s) in the woods.*

- **buffalo**: *I hope there aren't too many buffalo(e)(s) outside.*

- **squid**: *The squid(s) are amazing creatures.*

- **swine**: The plural is "swine" when referring to pigs, e.g. *"Swine are reared extensively in Europe."* When referring to people, the plural may be also "swines", e.g. *"Those swines spilled their drinks on my couch and now it's all dirty."*

Also note that many adjectives used to describe a nation or an ethnic group can be used as plural nouns (often with "the"), e.g.

> *The British are notorious in Europe for their terrible cuisine.*
> *They could learn a lot from the French.*
> *Nevertheless, most Chinese enjoy a different kind of cuisine.*

IRREGULAR PLURAL PATTERNS

Many words of Latin and Greek origin retain their original plural endings (i.e. the plurals are not formed by adding -s or -es). It is often impossible to tell the correct plural form of a word without knowing its etymology. Rather than memorizing long lists of irregular plurals, you should be aware of the existing patterns to be able to recognize them when you see a new word. The most common patterns are:

> -us → -i: *nucleus: nuclei; alumnus: alumni; stimulus: stimuli.*

Note that for many such words, both -i and -uses are acceptable, for example: cactus – cacti/cactuses, focus – foci/focuses.

> -is → -es: *axis: axes; analysis: analyses; oasis: oases; thesis: theses.*

Note: -is is pronounced /ɪs/, -es is pronounced /iːz/.

> -ix → ices: *appendix: appendices; index: indices; matrix: matrices.*

Note: Both -ices and -ixes are often acceptable, for example index – indices/indexes.

> -um → -a: *bacterium: bacteria; medium: media; datum: data.*

Note: "data" and "media" are often treated as singular mass nouns in modern English.

> -on → -a: *criterion: criteria; phenomenon: phenomena.*
>
> -us → -*ra: *corpus: corpora; genus: genera.*
>
> -a → -ae: *nebula: nebulae; vertebra: vertebrae.*

Note: Often both -ae and -as are acceptable: antenna – antennae/antennas; formula – formulae/formulas.

Furthermore, there are a few patterns which are not of Latin or Greek origin:

> **-oo-** → **-ee-**: *foot: feet; goose: geese; tooth: teeth.*
>
> **-ouse** → **ice**: *mouse: mice; louse: lice.*

Note also the noun "**ox**" whose plural is "**oxen**".

SINGULAR NOUNS ENDING IN 's'

Many English nouns end with an "s" in their singular form. Most of these don't pose any problem; few people would say "these kiss were beautiful" instead of "these kisses". However, there are a few that are commonly misunderstood as being plural by learners:

news

Although the equivalent expression in many languages would be in the plural, "news" is a singular noun, so you would say:

> *The news is being broadcast by all major TV stations. (correct)*
> *The news are being broadcast by all major TV stations. (wrong)*

Oddly enough, "news" is uncountable, which means that not only do we use a singular verb after it, but you can't say "a news":

> *I've got good news. (correct)*
> *I've got a good news. (wrong)*

lens

Unlike "news", "lens" is countable, so you can try to remember that if there can be "two lenses", there must also be "one lens":

His new lens is big. (correct)
His new lens are big. (wrong)

series

To make things even more confusing, the plural of "series" is also series. You should therefore use a singular verb if you speak about one particular series, e.g.

My favourite TV series has been cancelled.

and a plural verb if you speak about several series at a time, e.g.

All the series on the Unknown Channel are good.

means

Just like "series", "means" is already both the singular and the plural form of the noun. For example:

Railway is a means [singular] of transportation, but there are also several other good means [plural] of transportation.

bellows

Bellows is an instrument used for blowing air. Like "series", the plural of "bellows" is also "bellows", so you have to use a singular verb when speaking about one bellows and a plural verb when speaking about more than one.

measles

Measles is a disease, and as you have probably noticed from the previous sentence, the word is in the singular:

Measles is especially common among children. (correct)
Measles are especially common among children. (wrong)

Quite naturally, it is uncountable, i.e. you cannot have "two measles".

species

Species (pronounced /ˈspiːʃiːz/, sometimes also /ˈspiːsiːz/) is defined in biology as the largest group of organisms capable of interbreeding and producing a fertile offspring (although there are also exceptions to this definition). The plural is also "species", e.g.

> *The domestic cat is a species [singular] of the Felidae family. The lion and the jaguar are two other species [plural] belonging to the same family.*

Christmas

Christmas is a singular noun, and as such it takes a singular verb:

> *Christmas is a great time of year. (correct)*
> *Christmas are a great time of year. (wrong)*

chess

The game of chess is singular in English:

> *Chess is an intellectually demanding game. (correct)*
> *Chess are an intellectually demanding game. (wrong)*

NOUNS THAT ONLY EXIST IN THE PLURAL

Finally, to finish our exhausting discussion on unusual plural forms, let's take a look at nouns that only have a plural form and may be therefore confusing for some learners if the equivalent expression in their mother tongue is in the singular:

jeans, tights, trousers, pants, panties

All this hosiery is used only in the plural, usually because they come in pairs (for both legs), and the singular form has died out:

> *Her new jeans/tights/trousers/pants/panties are black. (correct)*
> *Her new jeans/tights/trousers/pants/panties is black. (wrong)*

It is common to refer to these as a "pair", for example:

> *I bought a new pair of jeans.*

Note that the word "trousers" in British English means any kind of clothes worn from the waist down covering both legs separately, whereas the general term in the US is "pants" (and "trousers" is used only for specific kinds of "pants"). In British English "pants" means the same as "underpants" or "knickers", i.e. a kind of underwear. These are commonly referred to also as "panties" in American English.

tongs, scissors, pliers, glasses, binoculars

Not to be confused with "thongs" (the plural of "thong" which is a type of underwear), tongs, a tool for gripping and lifting things, are also used in the plural, along with similar tools which come in pairs:

> *The tongs/scissors/pliers are not big enough. (correct)*
> *The tongs/scissors/pliers is not big enough. (wrong)*

Other nouns that somehow represent an inseparable pair also usually exist only in the plural, e.g. glasses, binoculars. Just like for hosiery, it is common to refer to all these using the word "pair":

> *Peter has just got two new pairs of glasses.*

Other examples

There are many other examples of nouns that exist only in the plural. Some of the more common are:

- **clothes** (not to be confused with cloths)
- **remains** (the rests of something)
- **goods** (items intended for sale)
- **stairs** (we say "one step" rather than "one stair")
- **arms** (in the sense of "weapons")
- **outskirts** (of a city)
- **shenanigans** (mischief, craziness, trickery)

ARE THINGS HE, SHE, OR IT?

Unlike most other European languages, Modern English has no grammatical genders. When we speak about an inanimate object, we always refer to it as "it". For example:

This is a stone. It is very heavy. (correct)
This is a stone. He is very heavy. (wrong)

This is a flower. It is red. (correct)
This is a flower. She is red. (wrong)

Although animals are animate, an animal is also traditionally referred to as "it", unless you want to emphasize its sex or your personal relationship with it:

I saw a stray dog. It was large. (correct)
I saw a stray dog. He/she was large. (see below)

In this case, since the animal's sex doesn't matter and we have no personal relationship with it, we would use "it". Note, however, that it is customary to refer to all animals as "he" or "she" in certain circles, especially among animal rights activists and vegans.

Nevertheless, most people would use "he" or "she" (depending on the sex of the animal) only when referring to an animal with whom they have a close personal relationship:

> *The dachshund is a member of our family. She is always so curious.*

Of course, using "it" is completely correct too:

> *The dachshund is a member of our family. It is always so curious.*

Sometimes things are referred to as "she" to show affection. It is traditional for ships to be a "she":

> *What a ship! She's been cruising the sea for fifty years and still looks like new.*

but it is not wrong to refer to a ship in an impersonal manner as "it". Similarly, countries and cars are sometimes referred to as "she":

> *I love Great Britain. She is beautiful.*
> *Let's try out our new Ferrari. She's ready for it.*

However, don't overdo it. Even if you really love your Ferrari, referring to it always as "she" may make you sound pretentious or snobbish.

United States is/are

The United States has always been causing (grammatical) trouble... or *have* been? "The United States" was treated as a plural noun in most of the 19th century, but the usage shifted during the 20th century towards treating it as a singular noun.

In other words, we understand "The United States" as "the country consisting of united states" in modern English and use singular verbs after it, as in

> *The United States has a very aggressive foreign policy. (correct)*
> *The United States have a very aggressive foreign policy. (obsolete)*

We can see the singular United States also in the following witticism:

> *The United States invariably does the right thing, after having exhausted every other alternative.*
>
> — Winston Churchill

SEVERAL THOUSAND(S) OF

The words "hundred", "thousand", "million", and so on, when they are used in counting objects, are *always in the singular* and usually not followed by "of", for example

> *There were two thousand people. (correct)*
> *There were two thousands people. (wrong)*
> *There were two thousands of people. (wrong)*

A number is only followed by "of" when we enumerate something else than a noun, for example:

> *We ordered five hundred of these. (correct)*
> *We ordered five hundred these. (wrong)*

Also note that, when speaking about the number of objects or people, we usually say "a hundred/thousand/million", rather than "one hundred/thousand/million".

The only case when "hundred", "thousand", etc., take the plural form is when they are used in the sense of "an unspecified number of hundreds/thousands/...", e.g.

> *Millions long for immortality who don't know what to do with themselves on a rainy Sunday afternoon.*
>
> —Susan Ertz

If there is a noun after "hundreds", "thousands", etc., we use "of":

> *Thousands of people were left homeless after the floods.*

What do we do when we want to use "several", "many", "a few", etc., instead of a number? Some speakers do say "several hundreds/thousands/... of" but the variant without "-s" and "of" is much more common and considered acceptable by all speakers, whereas the other variant is usually considered unnatural by those who don't use it. It is therefore advisable to stick to the singular form:

> *There were several thousand people. (correct)*
> *There were several thousands of people. (less natural)*

DOT, PERIOD, FULL STOP, POINT

These four terms can be quite confusing for native speakers of other languages because they usually don't correspond well to the terms used in their mother tongue.

The distinction is actually rather simple. The little dot which you can find at the end of a sentence is called *period* in American English and *full stop* in British English, even when you "pronounce" the full stop for emphasis; for example, a father arguing with his daughter could say:

You are not going out with Zack, period. [American English]
You are not going out with Zack, full stop. [British English]

The term *dot* is used when pronouncing the character in domain names; for example, "www.google.com" would be pronounced

"Double U double U double U dot google dot com"

A funny thing to notice here is that WWW is an abbreviation of "World Wide Web" that contains three times more syllables in its spoken form than the term it is supposed to abbreviate.

Finally, the term *point* refers to the dot used in numbers to separate the fractional part from the integer part (unlike many other languages, English uses a decimal point, not a decimal comma). The numbers after the decimal point are pronounced in isolation, e.g.

3.14 = "three point one four"
36.952 = "thirty six point nine five two"
0.25 = "zero point two five", or just .25 = "point two five"

A COUPLE (OF)

Although it is quite common to hear expressions like "in a couple hours" and "I saw a couple people" in spoken American English (but not so much in British English), in formal written English (on both sides of the Atlantic), the form with "of" is the only one considered appropriate, for example:

We will leave in a couple of days. (correct)
We will leave in a couple days. (colloquial)

There is one phrase, however, in which "a couple" is always used without "of", namely "a couple more". For example:

I need a couple more cups of coffee. (correct)

I need a couple of more cups of coffee. (wrong)

IN/ON (THE) I/INTERNET

The English word "Internet" is problematic for English learners because it can cause several problems at once. First, when it is used as a noun describing *the* network we all use, it is used with the definite article:

I love the Internet! (correct)

I love Internet! (dubious)

I wrote "dubious" instead of "wrong" for the second option because some native speakers do use the noun without the article. However, most English speakers consider the first option to be the only correct one, so it is the one you should use.

The word "Internet" isn't preceded by an article when it is used as an adjective in front of a noun that itself has no article, e.g.

Do you have Internet access? (correct)

Do you have the Internet access? (wrong)

The term "Internet access" is sometimes shortened to "Internet", in which case we *don't* use an article:

Do you have Internet? (correct, informal)

Do you have the Internet? (wrong)

The second sentence doesn't make sense; you can't *own* the Internet, but you can have Internet in the sense of Internet access.

Another problem is the preposition. When something is part of the Internet, we say that it is "on the Internet", not "in" or "at" the Internet:

> *I didn't find the article on the Internet. (correct)*
> *I didn't find the article in the Internet. (wrong)*

As for whether you should capitalize "Internet": It's hard to make a mistake here. Both "Internet" and "internet" are commonly used when referring to the network. Traditionally, "Internet" was considered a proper noun and written with a capital letter. Nowadays, the noun is considered to be a generic name, like "electricity" or "water supply", and is commonly spelled "internet", so:

> *You can surf the Internet. (correct, more traditional)*
> *You can also surf the internet. (correct, more recent)*

Some style guides prefer one spelling to the other, so if you are writing a text for someone else, you may want to check which style guide they follow.

SUB(S)TRACT

I have heard a lot of people using the word "substract" and its derived form "substraction". Long story short, the correct forms are **"subtract"** and **"subtraction"** (without an "s").

The reason why so many English learners make the mistake is probably that there is a corresponding word in many languages that does contain an "s", e.g. *soustraire* in French or *sustraer* in Spanish. Another reason might be that learners confuse its sound with "abstract", a relatively common word that contains the letter group "bstract", not just "btract".

You and I/me

Should you always write and say "you and I" and avoid "you and me"? Some native speakers will tell you so. Not only does no such rule exist, but using "you and I" instead of "you and me" is wrong in many cases.

The rule is quite simple, actually. If "you and I" is the subject of a sentence (i.e. "you and I" are the people who are doing the action), it is the correct form:

> *You and I are good friends. (correct)*
> *You and me are good friends. (colloquial)*

The second example is not *wrong* (it is widespread to use "you and me" this way); it's just colloquial and should be avoided in formal speech and writing.

If "you and I" is an object (i.e. the people to *whom* something is being done), the correct form is "you and me":

> *She didn't see you and me. (correct)*
> *She didn't see you and I. (wrong)*

A simple mnemonic is to say "he" or "him" instead of "you". Would you say "she didn't see him and I"? I don't think so.

Native speakers are usually taught they shouldn't use "you and me" as the subject of a sentence in formal writing. Many of these misunderstand the rule as "never use you and me" and even "correct" other people who say, for example, "she sees you and me", claiming it should be "she sees you and I".

You may safely ignore such "advice". It is possible that "you and I" as an object will become so widespread to be considered an acceptable variant in the future, but it is certainly not acceptable now.

ALL/ANYTHING/EVERYTHING BUT

These three expressions are among the most confusing in the English language for native speakers of other languages. Although "all", "everything" and "anything" are all similar in meaning, when they are followed with "but", they mean completely different things!

All but

"All but" means (completely illogically, I agree) "almost", "nearly". For example,

> *He was all but lost in the city.*
> *It was all but impossible.*

could be expressed without using "all but" as

> *He was almost lost in the city.*
> *It was nearly impossible.*

Anything but

"Anything but" can be rephrased using "not at all" or "in no way". For example,

> *They were anything but positive about the proposition.*
> *This smartphone is anything but ordinary.*

which means the same as

> *They were not at all positive about the proposition.*
> *This smartphone is in no way ordinary.*

Everything but

The meaning of "everything but" is quite literal; it is synonymous with "everything except", "everything with the exception of". For example,

> *I eat everything but meat.*
> *She wants everything but happiness for other people.*

which means

> *I eat everything except meat.*
> *She wants everything with the exception of happiness for other people.*

INFORMATION(S) IS/ARE

There's nothing wrong with saying *Informationen* in German or *informations* in French, both being the plural forms of "information". In English, however, the word is uncountable, i.e. there is **no plural form of it**. The singular form already expresses the same idea as "informations" in other languages:

> *I don't have enough information. (correct)*
> *I don't have enough informations. (wrong)*

Uncountability of the word "information" also implies that you can't say "an information". If you want to express that you are speaking about "one information", you can use the expression "a piece of information".

> *That's an interesting piece of information. (correct)*
> *That's interesting information. (correct; notice no "an")*
> *That's an interesting information. (wrong)*

Names of numbers above 1000

First, we should note that there is a certain oddity in modern English in the nomenclature for numbers like "one thousand million", "one million million", etc. The modern English pattern differs from most of Europe (as well as from its earlier usage in English):

Number	Continental Europe	Modern English
10^6	*Million*	*Million*
10^9	*Milliard*	**Billion**
10^{12}	*Billion*	**Trillion**
10^{15}	*Billiard*	Quadrillion

As you can see, the Continental European convention is to alternate between -ion and -iard, whereas the modern English convention uses just the -ion suffix.

Another important difference in comparison to other European languages is that the words "hundred", "thousand", "million", etc., *are never used in the plural* when pronouncing the name of a number (in the same vein as there are no plurals when speaking about the number of some objects, as we saw earlier), for example:

> *seven thousand three hundred (and) fifty two (7,352) (correct)*
> *seven thousands three hundreds (and) fifty two (7,352) (wrong)*

> *two million one hundred thousand (2,100,000) (correct)*
> *two millions one hundred thousands (2,100,000) (wrong)*

We only use the plural ("hundreds, thousands, millions") when referring to an unspecified number of objects of the given order of magnitude. Compare:

Millions of locusts swarmed over the city.
Thirty million locusts swarmed over the city.

As to whether to use "and" between "hundred" and the rest of the number, both "two hundred and fifty" and "two hundred fifty" are correct. The variant with "and" is more common in British English whereas the variant without "and" is more common in American English.

Also note that, in the written form, orders can be separated using a comma, not a dot or a space, e.g. "2,100,000", not "2.100.000" or "2 100 000".

COLLECTIVE NOUNS

The word "majority" is one of a few nouns in English that can be used either with a singular or a plural verb form (i.e. both "majority is" and "majority are" are grammatically correct but carry a different meaning). These nouns are called *collective nouns* because they describe a *collective* (i.e. a *group*) of people or things. Their usage in English differs from most other languages; we use a singular verb if we mean the whole group as a single entity, and a plural verb if we mean all of the individuals who belong to the group. For example:

A majority of people don't want a war. (correct)
A majority of people doesn't want a war. (wrong)

Here we are obliged to use "don't" because we mean the people, not the "majority" itself. On the other hand, we would say

A majority of people is, by definition, a part of the population containing at least 50% of it. (correct)
A majority of people are, by definition, a part of the population containing at least 50% of it. (wrong)

because here we are referring to the "majority" itself, not to the individuals. The list of collective nouns includes, but is not limited to:

Audience, cabinet, committee, company, corporation, council, department, family, firm, group, jury, minority, navy, public, team.

For example, you can say "his family are all tall", when you mean "his family members are all tall". Note, however, that the usage of a plural verb after a collective noun denoting an institution (such as department, parliament, etc.) is much more widespread in British English than in American English; a Brit would likely say "the parliament *are* voting today" whereas an American would probably say "the congress *is* voting today".

A COUPLE OF ... ARE/IS

When learners see "a couple", which is in the singular, they assume the verb must be in the singular too. However, the same we've said about collective nouns applies to expressions like "a couple" and "a few" as well.

Although the noun itself is in the singular, what it really describes is more than just one thing or person. It doesn't matter whether you mean literally *a couple*, i.e. just two people or things, or you use "a couple of" synonymously to "a few"; it represents a plural idea, so the correct form is:

There were just a couple of people at the party. (correct)
There was just a couple of people at the party. (wrong)

Only when "a couple" is not followed by "of" and is used to mean "a pair of people", *and* you refer to the couple as a whole, not just to individual persons who constitute it, you should treat it as singular:

A couple in love is always a nice thing to see. (correct)
A couple in love are always a nice thing to see. (wrong)

PEOPLE ARE/IS

If you say "people is", you can be almost sure it is mistake. The word "people" is an irregular plural form of "person" (although the word "persons" also exists in English, it sounds very formal and is used primarily in legal contexts), and unlike some other languages (such as *la gente* in Spanish), it is a plural noun:

> *There are a lot of people at the party. (correct)*
> *There is a lot of people at the party. (wrong)*
> *There are a lot of persons at the party. (too formal)*

(Note that "a lot", just like "a couple", is treated as a collective noun and doesn't change the grammatical number in any way; we will explain that in more detail in the next section.) The same is true for any other verb, not just "to be":

> *People generally don't know much about mathematics. (correct)*
> *People generally doesn't know much about mathematics. (wrong)*
> *Persons generally don't know much about mathematics. (wrong)*

However, the word "people" has also another meaning, namely "the set of individuals who belong to the same ethnic group", i.e. something similar to "folk" or "nation". In this sense, it is usually used in the plural:

> *Ancient peoples of Central America often saw each other as an enemy. (correct)*
> *Ancient people of Central America often saw each other as an enemy. (probably wrong)*

The second example is not grammatically wrong; it would imply that the individual people (persons) saw each other as an enemy. If we mean that different tribes saw each other as an enemy, we must use "peoples".

In the very same sense, people could be used as a singular noun (but such usage is quite rare):

> *The Maya people was composed of distinct ethnic groups. (correct)*
> *The Maya people were composed of distinct ethnic groups. (wrong)*

Again, since we mean the whole Maya civilization, not just individuals, we have to use "people was". If you want to be on the safe side, you can use another word like "civilization", "tribe", or "population"; these are always used with a singular verb.

A LOT OF ... ARE/IS

When something has an indefinite article, i.e. "a" or "an", it is usually followed by a singular verb, for example "a tree is". However, "a lot of" is used in a way similar to collective nouns (like "a couple of"):

> *A lot of new trees have been planted in our town. (correct)*
> *A lot of new trees has been planted in our town. (wrong)*
>
> *There are a lot of students in the lecture hall. (correct)*
> *There is a lot of students in the lecture hall. (see below)*

Another way to look at this is that in English, unlike many other languages, the subject doesn't have to be in the nominative (grammatically, "of trees" is in the genitive). In the first sentence above, you should ask yourself, "What has been planted?" Since the answer is "new trees" and you would say "new trees have", that's the verb form you should use, regardless of what precedes the noun.

Note to the usage of "there is/are": "There is + plural noun" is considered wrong by most speakers, but using "there's + plural" is quite common in spoken language. This tendency seems to be quite natural, considering there is usually only one version of the corresponding expression in other languages, e.g. *il y a* in French and *es gibt* in German.

"A lot of" can be used also for uncountable nouns, i.e. nouns describing a substance or a material, such as "water", "sand", "iron", etc. In this case, since the noun is in the singular, so is the verb:

> *A lot of water is being wasted every day. (correct)*
> *A lot of water are being wasted every day. (wrong)*

MANY, MUCH, A LOT OF, AND LOTS OF

These four phrases, "many", "much", "a lot of", and "lots of", all express a similar idea of a large amount of something, but they are not completely interchangeable. The first important difference is that "many" can be used only with countable nouns in the plural (e.g. "many trees", "many houses", "many people"), and "much" can only be used with uncountable (mass) nouns in the singular (e.g. "much water", "much wood", "much happiness"), for example:

> *There's not much water in the swimming pool. (correct)*
> *There's not many water in the swimming pool. (wrong)*
>
> *There are many people in the crowd. (correct)*
> *There are much people in the crowd. (wrong)*

There is no such distinction for "a lot of" and "lots of", which can be used with both, i.e. both "a lot of/lots of people" and "a lot of/lots of water" are correct. Don't forget what you learned in the last section, i.e. that when "a lot of" is used with a plural noun, the verb is in the plural too, even though "a lot" itself is in the singular:

> *A lot of people don't know the word "onychophagia". (correct)*
>
> *A lot of people doesn't know the word "onychophagia". (wrong)*

In a similar fashion, "lots of" with a singular noun is used with a singular verb:

> *Lots of water is being wasted every day. (correct)*
>
> *Lots of water are being wasted every day. (wrong)*

Again, the right way to think about the expression is to ask "what is being wasted?" Since the answer is "water" (a singular noun), the verb is in the singular as well.

Difference in register

The most important difference between "many"/"much" and "a lot of"/"lots of" is that the latter can't be used when asking about an amount ("how much", "how many") and, usually, when used in connection with another word ("too many, "as much as", "so many"):

> *How many people were there? (correct)*
>
> *How a lot of people were there? (wrong)*
>
> *We have as much money as they have. (correct)*
>
> *We have as lots of money as they have. (wrong)*

Nevertheless, note that "a lot more/fewer/less" is completely acceptable in informal communication.

In virtually all other situations, "many"/"much", "a lot of" and "lots of" mean essentially the same, but there is an important difference in register. "Many" and "much" sound quite formal, "a lot of" is informal, and "lots of" is even less formal:

> *There are many people at the party. (very formal)*
> *There are a lot of people at the party. (informal)*
> *There are lots of people at the party. (even more informal)*

"Many" and "much" in affirmative (positive) sentences (like the one above) sound so formal you will almost never hear these in a normal conversation; you should mostly use them in writing.

In negative sentences, however, "many" and "much" sound quite natural even in normal speech; there is nothing wrong with saying, for example:

> *I don't have much money. (fine in formal and informal contexts)*
> *I don't have a lot of money. (fine in an informal context)*
> *I don't have lots of money. (even more informal)*

IS A DOCTOR HE OR SHE?

Traditionally, in English, when you had to use a pronoun for a person whose sex was unknown because it had been previously referred to using a term like "child", "doctor", "researcher", etc., you would say "he", "him", "his", or "himself" (depending on the context). For example:

> *Take care of your child. His life depends on you.*
>
> *You should see a doctor. He will know what to do.*
>
> *Every researcher has asked himself at some point of his career whether his contribution to science was good enough.*

Although the pronouns were masculine, the child in the first example could be a girl, and the doctor and the researcher could be women. However, this usage is now becoming outdated, as it is seen as stimulating gender inequality. There are several options to mitigate the issue. You can use "he or she" instead of "he":

> *Take care of your child. His or her life depends on you.*

You should see a doctor. He or she will know what to do.

Every researcher has asked himself or herself at some point of his or her career whether his or her contribution to science was good enough.

As you can see especially in the third example, this grammatical tool soon becomes clumsy if you use it too often. Another possibility is to reword the whole sentence using the corresponding plural nouns, but this doesn't always work:

Take care of your children. Their lives depend on you.

~~You should see doctors. They will know what to do.~~

All researchers have asked themselves at some point of their career whether their contribution to science was good enough.

Finally, it is becoming increasingly widespread and regarded as completely grammatically correct to use a plural pronoun for a singular noun to refer to it in a gender-neutral way:

Take care of your child. Their life depends on you.

You should see a doctor. They will know what to do.

Every researcher has asked themselves at some point of their career whether their contribution to science was good enough.

Such sentences may sound odd at first because they seemingly break the most elementary grammatical rules. However, there seems to be an inevitable trend for this usage to completely replace the gender-neutral "he, his, him" in English.

Note that some authors went as far as to always use a *feminine* pronoun, for example:

Every researcher has asked herself at some point of her career whether her contribution to science was good enough.

even though they refer to male researchers as well. Please, don't do that. It is unnecessary and confusing, unless you do indeed mean only female researchers.

EACH OTHER'S OR EACH OTHERS'

You've certainly heard phrases like "to hold each other's hand", but where to put the apostrophe in these in their written form? Long story short, the correct spelling is the one used in the previous sentence, i.e. *each other's*. Another example:

> *We didn't see each other's face. (correct)*
> *We didn't see each others' face. (wrong)*

This is quite logical. The possessive form in English is formed by adding *'s* at the and of a noun, unless it is a plural noun, in which case we write just an apostrophe, e.g.

> *This boy's girlfriend ... (correct, singular)*
> *These boys' girlfriends ... (correct, plural)*

This rules out *each others*, as the possessive apostrophe must be there. In the case of "each other", "other" is in the singular, because it's after "each"—you wouldn't say "each boys" instead of "each boy", would you. By adding the possessive *'s*, we get the correct form *each other's*.

MATTER/QUESTION OF TIME

The equivalent to the phrase "a matter/question of time" in most European languages is literally "a question of time", e.g. *una cuestión de tiempo* in Spanish or *eine Frage der Zeit* in German. In English, both "a matter of time" and "a question of time" are acceptable, but the phrase "a question of time" is slowly falling out of fashion.

The difference is even more pronounced in connection with "just" which is nowadays only rarely used with "a question of time":

> *It's just a matter of time. (correct)*
> *It's just a question of time. (dated)*

IN (THE) CASE OF

Whether to use "the" in "in (the) case" depends on the intended meaning. "In case of" is synonymous with "in the event of", for example:

> *In case of fire, please call the fire department. (correct)*
> *In the case of fire, please call the fire department. (wrong)*
>
> *In case of earthquake, leave the building. (correct)*
> *In the case of earthquake, leave the building. (wrong)*

"In case" can be used also without "of" in the phrase "just in case", which means "just to be safe if something bad happened":

> *It's dangerous outside. I'll take my gun with me, just in case.*

The phrase "in the case of" (with the definite article) is usually used in the meaning "regarding", "in the matter of", "in relation to":

> *I know that you have always been faithful, but in the case of your husband, I wouldn't be so sure. (correct)*
> *I know that you have always been faithful, but in case of your husband, I wouldn't be so sure. (wrong)*

TON OR TONNE

In English, "ton" refers to the unit used in the US defined as 1 ton = 2,000 pounds = 907 kg. It can also refer to the ton used in the UK where 1 ton = 2,240 pounds = 1,016 kg, but which is no longer officially used (since 1985). If you want to refer to the so called "metric ton", the word you are looking for is pronounced the same but is spelled "tonne", i.e. 1 tonne = 1000 kg.

ON (THE) ONE HAND

Both "on the one hand" and "on one hand" are considered correct by most dictionaries, but "on <u>the</u> one hand" is much more common:

> *On the one hand, I really wanted to come. On the other hand, I hated all the people who would be coming with me. (correct)*
>
> *On one hand, I really wanted to come. On the other hand, I hated all the people who would be coming with me. (considered unnatural by some)*

Intuitively, the first "the" seems illogical because you are referring to one of your hands without specifying which one. You wouldn't say, for example, "I wore a glove on the one hand and nothing on the other one", unless you were waving one of your hands in front of you while saying that.

I've read an explanation that the first "the" indeed does originate in gesticulating with one of your hands while saying the phrase—that is, you would look at your hand and say "on the *one* hand ...". Whether this is the real etymology, we may never know.

Advice(s) is/are

Slightly surprisingly, "advice" is uncountable in English, and as such there is no plural form of it:

> *His advice was very helpful. (correct)*
> *His advices were very helpful. (wrong)*

Since it is uncountable, we cannot say "an advice". We would usually say simply "advice" (without an article), or "piece of advice":

> *This was good advice. (correct)*
> *This was a good piece of advice. (correct)*
> *This was a good advice. (wrong)*

Money is/are

Just like water, sugar, or love, *money* (in its most common sense) is an uncountable noun. This means, in particular, that we can't have "a money", which would be the same as saying that we have "one money"; you can have "one dollar", for example, but "one money" doesn't really make sense.

However, just like other mass nouns, "money" is always used with a singular verb. Just like we would say "the sugar is on the table" (not "the sugar *are*"), we would use "is" with money too:

> *The money is on the table. (correct)*
> *The money are on the table. (wrong)*

Also, "many money" is incorrect, since "many" means "a large number of", so we have to use "much" (or "a lot of" or another expression which can be used both with countable and uncountable nouns). For example:

> *My parents don't have much money. (correct)*
> *My parents don't have a lot of money. (correct)*
> *My parents don't have many money. (wrong)*

However, just like water, sugar, and love, money can be used as a countable noun to express a slightly different idea. Just like the British *waters* may be dangerous, you can put three *sugars* in your coffee, and many people have several great *loves* in their lives, "moneys" or "monies" (the possible plural forms of money) may be used to talk about several sources of money. Nevertheless, such usage is mostly limited to legal contexts, and using the word "moneys" in an everyday conversation would make you sound unnatural.

THE PERSON WHO/THAT ...

Many English speakers believe there's a rule in English that you can't use "that" when speaking about a person, as in "the waiter that served me was really friendly". Even though examples of breaking the rule can be found as early as in the works of Chaucer and Shakespeare, it is advisable for a learner to follow it; if all English speakers consider using "who" for a person acceptable, but many consider using "that" to be a mistake, it is better to use the variant acceptable by all, isn't it? For example:

> *The waiter who served me was really friendly. (correct)*
> *The waiter that served me was really friendly. (discouraged)*
>
> *The man who stole the car was arrested. (correct)*
> *The man that stole the car was arrested. (discouraged)*

ECONOMICS OR ECONOMY

The **economy** is, according to the Oxford Learner's Dictionary, "the relationship between production, trade and the supply of money in a particular country or region", so we can say, for example:

> *The economy is in recession.*

Economics is a science that studies economies and develops possible models for their functioning, e.g.

> *He studied economics at the LSE (London School of Economics).*

Economic, without an "s", is an adjective meaning "connected with economy", e.g.

> *The economic growth is very slow.*

Economical, on the other hand, carries a somewhat figurative meaning of "not requiring too much of something" (such as money, space, time, etc.), e.g.

> *That placement of furniture exhibits a very economical use of space.*

10 DOLLARS IS/ARE

When we speak about a specific sum of money or about a price, we usually treat it as singular:

> *10 dollars is too much for that. (correct)*
> *10 dollars are too much for that. (unnatural)*

You can think about "10 dollars" as being short for "the amount of 10 dollars" or "the price of 10 dollars". Since we would say "the amount is" and "the price is", "[the amount/price of] 10 dollars is" is also correct.

However, whether to treat it as being singular or plural depends on whether you think about the money as about the sum or as about the individual coins or banknotes:

> *I just got 5 euros. I gave it [the amount] to my mum. (correct)*
> *I just got 5 euros. I gave them [the individual euros] to my mum.*
> *(possible)*

Nevertheless, this only makes sense when speaking about physical money and not something abstract like a price. When you talk about electronic money, using "it" is the only natural choice:

> *He transferred £44.95 to my account, but it hasn't arrived yet. (cor.)*
> *He transferred £44.95 to my account, but they haven't arrived yet.*
> *(wrong)*

Mistakes with verbs and tenses

WORD ORDER IN SUBORDINATE CLAUSES

Word order in subordinate clauses, i.e. parts of sentences beginning with "the place where ...", "the time when ...", "the man who ...", etc., is not the same as in questions. Word order in subordinate clauses is **exactly the same** as in ordinary indicative (non-question) sentences, e.g.

> *I don't know why he goes there. (correct)*
> *I don't know why does he go there. (wrong)*
>
> *She didn't tell me where she hid it. (correct)*
> *She didn't tell me where did she hide it. (wrong)*
>
> *We all know why Peter has never gone there. (correct)*
> *We all know why has Peter never gone there. (wrong)*

The same word order is preserved even if the whole sentence (but not the clause) is a question:

> *Do you know why she did it? (correct)*
> *Do you know why did she do it? (wrong)*
>
> *Do you know why he is acting so strange? (correct)*
> *Do you know why is he acting so strange? (wrong)*

"But isn't word order different in questions?", you are perhaps asking. It is, but the question is "Do you know …?". The "why she did it" part is a subordinate clause.

People tend to make mistakes especially after "who" and "what" in connection with "be":

Do you know who he is? (correct)
Do you know who is he? (wrong)

Do you know what it is? (correct)
Do you know what is it? (wrong)

The structure is slightly different when "who" or "what" is the subject of the sentence, but the word order is still the same:

Do you know who did it? (correct)
Do you know who did do it? (wrong)

PRESENT PERFECT WITH SPECIFIC TIME

The present perfect expresses the idea of "an action that was finished at some unspecified point in the past". Saying "I have done it yesterday" is basically the same as saying "I finished doing it yesterday at some unspecified point in the past". It doesn't really work, does it; it's either "at some point" or "yesterday", not both. If you want to include the time when the action took place, you must use the simple past tense (the "-ed" form), e.g.

I did it yesterday. (correct)
I have done it yesterday. (wrong)

I visited my grandmother last weekend. (correct)
I have visited my grandmother last weekend. (wrong)

However, the simple past is ambiguous. "I did it yesterday" can be used to express that you finished it yesterday as well as that you left the work unfinished and will continue doing it later, e.g. "I did it yesterday, and I am also going to do it tomorrow". If you want to express that the action is already completed, you can use verbs like "finish" or "complete" in the simple past:

> *I finished my homework yesterday. (correct)*
> *I have finished my homework yesterday. (wrong)*

A strong indicator that you shouldn't use the present perfect is the presence of "when" in the sentence, since "when" always refers to a specific point in time:

> *When did you write the book? (correct)*
> *When did you finish writing the book? (correct)*
> *When have you written the book? (wrong)*
>
> *I don't know when she did her homework. (correct)*
> *I don't know when she finished her homework. (correct)*
> *I don't know when she has done her homework. (wrong)*

Note that there is one case when "when + present perfect" can be used: to express surprise or mistrust. Say, a friend of yours told you how he enjoyed the view from the Eiffel Tower, and you weren't aware of the fact that he had ever been to Paris. You could ask

> *When have you been to Paris?*

It is an expression of surprise. You aren't really asking when he visited Paris; you express that the fact he did surprised you.

There is another common situation in which the rule can be (seemingly) broken. For example, it is perfectly fine to say:

> *How many films have you seen this week?*

The reason is that "this week" is not a point in the past (even though it *includes* days which are in the past); it is a point (a period) in the present. The present perfect in such a situation implies "so far": "How many films have you seen *so far (up until now)* this week?"

The present perfect can be used with any period which includes the present with the implied meaning of "so far". This includes the common adverbs students learn to use with the present perfect, e.g. "ever" ("from the beginning of the universe until now"), "never" ("not ever"), "already"/"yet" ("from some implied point in the past until now"), for example:

> *Have you done it yet?*
> *I have never been there.*

AREN'T I, AMN'T I

When you ask affirmative questions (the so called *question tags*) at the end of a sentence, you are supposed to use a contracted version of "be", "have", "do", etc., for example:

> *He is from England, <u>isn't he</u>?*
> *You have done your homework already, <u>haven't you</u>?*
> *You went on a holiday last week, <u>didn't you</u>?*

There is no problem with contracted forms of all the verbs, with one exception. What if you were to say: "I am new here, ...n't I?" What would the ellipsis (the three dots) stand for?

Unless you were in Scotland, people would find it funny if you said "amn't I" ("amn't" is a word that simply doesn't exist in any standard form of English). This (seemingly) leaves us with only one option—not contracting the verb at all:

> *I am new here, am I not?*

However, this puts strong, authoritative emphasis on the preceding statement and sounds very formal. For example, a teacher arguing with a disrespectful pupil could say

> *I believe I am your teacher, am I not?*

Because of this authoritative connotation, another way of saying "am I not" developed: virtually all native speakers use the form "aren't I", which is now completely acceptable in any spoken or informal written context. To sum it up:

> *I am new here, aren't I? (correct in any informal context)*
> *I am new here, am I not? (correct, but only in a fairly formal context)*
> *I am new here, amn't I? (incorrect; used only in a handful of dialects)*

USE TO DO

English learners learn quite early to use the phrase "someone used to do something". It expresses that someone did something regularly long time ago but doesn't do it anymore in the present. For example:

> *I used to play the violin.*

which means

> *I played the violin when I was younger, but I don't do that anymore.*

Learners often incorrectly infer that this is just the past tense of "I use to do", which should, logically, mean "I regularly do". However, **no such phrase exists** in standard English. Native speakers never say "I use to do something", however logical it may sound:

I used to play the violin. (correct, past)

I regularly play the violin. (correct, present)

I use to play the violin. (wrong)

Note, however, that native speakers quite often write "use to" as a misspelling of "used to", because "-d t-" is usually pronounced just as "t". When you see a native speaker write "I use to do", they mean, in fact, "I used to do".

HAVEN'T/DON'T HAVE

The verb "have" is slightly confusing because it has a negative form of its own. In standard modern English usage, the form "haven't" is used only as an auxiliary verb, e.g.

I haven't done it yet.

It is rarely used when there is a direct object, and such usage is considered colloquial:

She doesn't have a car. (correct)

She hasn't a car. (colloquial)

Such usage is slowly dying out, so it is advisable for a learner to avoid it altogether. If you want to use the word "haven't", there's a perfectly fine way to do that; simply add "got":

She hasn't got a car. (correct)

There are a few idioms in which "haven't" used as an ordinary verb has survived, however. The expression "I haven't a clue" was in fact even more common than "I don't have a clue" in American English until about 1990s, and it is still more popular in British English:

I haven't a clue. (correct)
I have no clue. (correct)
I don't have a clue. (correct)

Similarly, "haven't" is often used in connection with "idea", e.g.

I haven't the foggiest idea. (correct)
I haven't the faintest idea. (correct)

The former can be abbreviated to (with the same meaning):

I haven't the foggiest.

LEND OR BORROW

The verbs "lend" and "borrow" are among the most commonly confused words in the English language. Why? Because they are often translated by just a single verb into other languages. To put it completely bluntly:

to lend = to give something to somebody,
to borrow = to receive something from somebody,

provided the thing in question is expected to be returned to its original owner later. A simple way to decide whether to use "lend" or "borrow" is to see whether the sentence would make sense if we used "give" or "receive" instead. For example:

I lent him my new bicycle. (correct)
I borrowed him my new bicycle. (wrong)

Since you *give*, you *lend*, not borrow. Similarly:

Would you please lend me your bicycle? (correct)
Would you please borrow me your bicycle? (wrong)

"Would you please receive me your bicycle?" doesn't make any sense, whereas "Would you please give me your bicycle?" is perfectly fine. An example in the opposite direction:

I went to the bank to borrow some money. (correct)
I went to the bank to lend some money. (wrong)

Again, "I went to the bank to receive some money" is a perfectly fine sentence. The other sentence is probably wrong, unless you are Bill Gates and the bank wants to borrow money *from* you.

To loan or not to loan

The word loan is a noun describing either the act of lending something or, in the case of money, the money itself, e.g.

I got a loan from the bank.

In American English, "loan" can be used also as a verb synonymous to "lend" (mostly in connection with money):

A friend of mine loaned me a lot of money. (American English)

However, you will probably get a few strange looks if you try to use "loan" as a verb synonymous to "lend" in Europe, so it is better to avoid it when addressing an international audience.

BORING OR BORED

My mother once asked me how to use words like "bored" and "boring", "annoyed" and "annoying", etc. Oddly enough, her teacher told her a rule (which was *wrong*) that "-ed" words were used with people and "-ing" words were used with things.

The logic is as follows: Adjectives containing -ing or -ed are usually derived from verbs. If you say that someone is "-ing", it means *he himself* does the action described by the verb. If he is "-ed", someone or something does or did the action *to him*.

The verb "to annoy" means (roughly) "to make somebody angry". So, if someone is "annoying", *he or she* makes other people angry; if someone is "annoyed", other people or things made *him or her* angry. Similarly, the verb "bore" means "to make tired" (in a certain way), so if you say "I am boring", it means *you make* other people tired; if you say "I am bored", something *makes you* tired.

It works this way for any verb. The reason why my mother was told the rule was probably that for a lot of verbs (such as "to bore"), saying that a thing is "-ed" doesn't really make sense (it's hard to make a stone bored, for example). Nevertheless, it does make sense for many verbs (a stone can be breaking something as well as broken), and the logic is always the same.

MAKE SOMEONE (TO) DO SOMETHING

When you convince or force someone to do something, you can say that you "made him or her do it", without "to":

> *His mother made him clean his room. (correct)*
> *His mother made him to clean his room. (wrong?)*

The latter example is not grammatically wrong, but it would mean that "his mother created him (i.e. gave birth to him) in order to clean his room," which is probably not a thing we would normally want to say.

LEARN SOMEONE TO DO SOMETHING

In English, when you improve your own knowledge, you *learn*, but when you increase someone's knowledge, you *teach*. For example:

> *My mother taught me to swim. (correct)*
> *My mother learned me to swim. (wrong)*

You can "make someone learn", but you can't "learn him or her". Even if the teacher and the learner are the same person, we still have to use "teach":

> *I teach myself to play the guitar. (correct)*
> *I learn to play the guitar by myself. (correct)*
> *I learn myself to play the guitar. (wrong)*

The moral is: Just remember that we never say "learn someone" in English.

'WILL' IN TIME CLAUSES

We never use the future tense in time clauses (introduced by words like "after", "as soon as", "before", etc.) in English. Should we need to express the idea of something happening after, before, etc., something else in the future, we use the present tense in the time clause and the future tense or a command in the main clause. For example:

> *I will give it to him after he arrives. (correct)*
> *I will give it to him after he will arrive. (wrong)*

> *As soon as you get the email, let me know, please. (correct)*
> *As soon as you will get the email, let me know, please. (wrong)*

When we use "when" as an adverb synonymous to "as soon as", the same rule as for other time clauses applies:

I'll call you when I come home. (correct)
I'll call you as soon as I come home. (correct)
I'll call you when I will come home. (wrong)

Send me an email when you arrive. (correct)
Send me an email as soon as you arrive. (correct)
Send me an email when you will arrive. (correct)

However, "when" can also mean "at what time". It doesn't introduce an adverbial time clause in this sense, and we *do use "will"* to express the future after it in this sense. Most importantly, we use it when asking questions:

When will you know the results? (correct)
At what time will you know the results? (correct)
When do you know the results? (wrong)

Things get a little complicated when the question is indirect (i.e. preceded by phrases like "could you tell me", "I'd like to ask you", etc.). The "when" part then looks like an adverbial time clause, but it is not. For example, if the direct question is:

When will you know the results?

we can ask:

Could you tell me when you will know the results? (correct)
Could you tell me at what time you will know the results? (correct)
Could you tell me when you know the results? (see below!)

The third sentence is grammatical, but it is a different question! In the first two cases, you ask when (i.e. *at what time*) the other person will know the results, so the answer would be something like "at 5 o'clock". In the other case, you ask the person to let you know *after* they get the results, so they would wait until they get them (e.g. until 5 o'clock) and then tell you, "I just got the results."

However, even in the sense of "at what time", it can make sense to use the present tense after "when". Compare:

> *I don't know when he will come.*
> *I don't know when he comes.*

The sentences could be rephrased as:

> *What I don't know is: When will he come?*
> *What I don't know is: At what time does he (habitually) come?*

Both questions are grammatically correct, but only the first one asks about the specific time when "he will come". The present tense in the other one indicates we ask about what happens *habitually* (such as every day or every week). The question is in the present because the answer would be in the present too, e.g. "He usually comes at 5 o'clock."

Finally, "when" can be sometimes used in the meaning of "because at that time":

> *I will go jogging at 5 a.m. when there will be no cars to bother me.*

The sentence is to be understood as:

> *I will go jogging at 5 a.m. because at that time there will be no cars to bother me.*

HE WANTS THAT I DO

If you want to express that someone wants "that someone else does something", the idiomatic way to do that in English is using the phrase "to want someone to do something". For example:

He wants me to go to his birthday party. (correct)
He wants that I go to his birthday party. (unnatural)

I don't want her to know about it. (correct)
I don't want that she know(s) about it. (unnatural)

Even though the grey examples make sense grammatically (the form used is the so called subjunctive mood, e.g. "that she know"; see the next section), they don't sound natural, perhaps because the present subjunctive is quite rare in modern English. Another example:

Don't you want me to come? (correct)
Don't you want that I come? (unnatural)

Note that "need", as a verb, follows the same pattern:

I need you to come to my office. (correct)
I need that you come to my office. (unnatural)

PRESENT SUBJUNCTIVE

The present subjunctive is a really easy mood to use: it is always identical to the infinitive. It is used after phrases like "It is important that", "I insist that", "It is necessary that", for example:

It is important that he be there next week. (correct)
It is important that he is there next week. (wrong)

The latter example doesn't really make sense, because "is" cannot be used with "next week". Sometimes, however, both the present tense and the subjunctive make sense and express a different idea. Compare:

> *It is important that he have a computer.*
> *It is important that he has a computer.*

The former sentence says that he is required to have a computer. The latter, on the other hand, says that he already has a computer, and this fact is important.

The present subjunctive does sound quite formal, and, as we saw in the case of "want" and "need", there is a tendency in English to replace it with the construction "for someone to do", especially in spoken language:

> *It is essential that he come early. (correct, very formal)*
> *It is essential for him to come early. (correct, preferred in speech)*

Sequence of tenses in indirect speech

This and the following two sections tackle perhaps the three most confusing topics in English grammar. If you feel overwhelmed at first, you can start reading the rest and return to this section when you feel like it (you don't have to master these topics in order to be able to read the rest of the book).

When we report an action that happened in the past, i.e. when we introduce a clause by phrases like "he said that" or "you told me that", we always describe the events from our current (present) point of view. For example, imagine you heard Adam say the following sentence:

> *I like chocolate.*

You want to report what he said, so you say:

Adam said that he <u>liked</u> chocolate. (correct)
Adam said that he likes chocolate. (wrong)

Notice how "liked" is in the past tense. Why? Because Adam liked chocolate in the past, when he told us that. We don't know if Adam still likes chocolate.

This is a hard concept to accept for those whose mother tongue does not follow the same logic. The best is probably to see it used in practice in a couple more examples:

What Jane said: *"I have to go to school."*

Jane said that she <u>had</u> to go to school. (correct)
Jane said that she has to go to school. (wrong)

What John said: *"I am going to send her an email."*

John said that he <u>was</u> going to send her an email. (correct)
John said that he is going to send her an email. (wrong)

What did John do? He did two things: He *said something*, and he *was going* to send an email to someone. There's no reason to change the tense when we add the word "that" between those two pieces of information.

What if John used the future tense instead? We just use the fact that the past tense of the verb "will" is "would" (which is a topic you will learn more about in the next section):

What John said: *"I will send her an email."*

John said that he <u>would</u> send her an email. (correct)
John said that he will send her an email. (wrong)

You will often hear that you are supposed to change the future tense to the conditional in reported speech, but in reality, we simply replace "will" with its past tense, just like we do with other verbs. Of course, you are free to choose whichever way is easier for you to remember.

When dealing with the present perfect, the logic stays absolutely the same: from "have done" we make "had done":

> What Mary said: *"I have finished my homework."*
>
> *Mary said that she <u>had</u> finished her homework. (correct)*
>
> *Mary said that she has finished her homework. (wrong)*

The last case that may cause confusion is when the original speaker already used the past tense. There is no "simple before-past tense" in English, so we make the "pastness" clear using the past perfect tense:

> What Richard said: *"I went to the cinema."*
>
> *Richard said that he <u>had gone</u> to the cinema. (correct)*
>
> *Richard said that he went to the cinema. (wrong)*

The latter example is grammatically correct, but it doesn't agree with what Richard said. It would only be accurate if Richard said: "I go to the cinema.".

If the speaker used the past perfect tense instead of the simple past (which would be quite unusual), there would be no room for making it even "paster", so we wouldn't change it at all. For example, if someone says "I had just turned off the TV", you would say "He said that he had just turned off the TV".

Exceptions

There are a few cases in which there is no shift. When the original speaker merely reports a general fact which is true now as it was then, we use the present tense in the dependent clause:

> What your teacher said: *"The Earth revolves around the Sun."*
>
> *My teacher said the Earth <u>revolves</u> around the Sun. (correct)*
>
> *My teacher said the Earth revolved around the Sun. (wrong)*

The past tense here would mean that the teacher implied the Earth revolved around the Sun only at that particular moment, which certainly is not the case.

If the speaker uses the conditional, it doesn't change either; a possibility or a wish in the past is still just a possibility or a wish in the present:

What Linda said: *"I would like to see my brother."*

Linda said that she <u>would</u> like to see her brother. (correct)

Linda said that she would have liked to see her brother. (wrong)

Other "modal" ideas follow the same pattern. "Could" stays "could", "should" stays "should", and "might" stays "might". However, in the case of could, we have the option to distinguish between the conditional ("would be able to") and between the past tense ("was able to") of "can". There's no change for the conditional:

What Gerald said: *"I could do that if I wanted."*

Gerald said that he <u>could</u> do that if he wanted. (correct)

Gerald said that he could have done that if he wanted. (wrong)

In the sense of the past tense of "can", it is possible to use "could", as well as "had been able to":

What Lara said: *"I could recite the poem yesterday."*

Lara said she <u>had been able to</u> recite the poem yesterday. (correct)

Lara said she <u>could</u> recite the poem yesterday. (correct)

The last case when the reported clause doesn't change is when the verb is in the subjunctive. We've already seen that in the example with Gerald: we used "if he wanted" instead of "if he had wanted" because wanted was in the past subjunctive (which we will discuss in more detail in the next section).

The present subjunctive doesn't change either:

What Tom said: *"My boss suggests that she come to the meeting."*

Tom said that his boss <u>suggested</u> that she <u>come</u> to the meeting. (cor.)

Tom said that his boss suggested that she came to the meeting. (wr.)

The future and the present tense

Are you afraid that we are going to have a lengthy discussion about reported speech in the future? Fortunately, you don't have to be. Reported speech in the future doesn't require any shift at all (and you will almost never need to use it anyway). For example:

What Anna will say: *"I work every day."*

Anna will say that she <u>works</u> every day. (correct)

Anna will say that she will work every day. (wrong)

The case of the present perfect tense ("he has said") may be a little surprising, but it has the word "present" in its name for a reason: there is no change of tenses after "has said":

What Linda has said: *"I need a new phone."*

Linda has said that she <u>needs</u> a new phone. (correct)

Linda has said that she needed a new phone. (wrong)

Linda has said that she has needed a new phone. (wrong)

THE CONDITIONAL

English conditional is one of the most common sources of mistakes for non-native speakers. Rather than starting a lengthy discussion about all possible forms and uses of the conditional, I will explain the three most common error patterns.

"If you will do this, I will do that."

Just like in time clauses, we don't use the future tense after "if" when we speak about future actions, which makes sense because the meaning of "if" is similar to the meaning of "when". The pattern is:

> *If something happens, someone will do something.*

For example:

> *If you <u>come</u> late, you will delay the whole project. (correct)*
> *If you will come late, you will delay the whole project. (wrong)*

However, "will" is not only an auxiliary verb of the future tense; it is also a modal verb meaning "be willing to", "be so good/kind as to". You may not have realized it, but you may have used it already in a couple of phrases. For example, when you say "Will you excuse me?", you aren't asking whether the other person is going to excuse you in the future; you are asking whether they are *willing to* excuse you right now (that is, whether they are *so kind as to* excuse you now).

As such, "will" is in the present tense, so there is no reason why it couldn't be used after "if", for example:

> *If you will excuse me, I must leave now.*

The structure is the same as in:

> *If you can excuse me, I must leave now.*

However, this is quite a special and relatively rare use. Remember: When you want to express an ordinary condition in the future, there is never "will":

> *If there <u>is</u> a storm tomorrow, we won't go to the beach. (correct)*
> *If there will be a storm tomorrow, we won't go to the beach. (wrong)*

"If you would do this, I would do that."

Just like we don't usually use "will" in future conditions, we rarely see its past tense ("would") in hypothetical conditions in the present. You can say, for example:

> If he <u>were</u> here, I would be so happy. (correct)
>
> If he would be here, I would be so happy. (probably wrong)

The form used after "if" in the example above is the so called *past subjunctive*. What that exactly means needn't trouble you; the important point to know is that it's the same *for every verb* as the simple past tense of that verb (e.g. "if I went", "if you did", "if he saw"), with the exception of "to be" for which it is "were" (e.g. "if I were", "if you were", "if he were"). Note, however, that many native speakers consider "was" an acceptable informal alternative for "I", "he", "she", and "it" as the subjunctive of the verb "be".

The subjunctive mood describes an action that (theoretically) could be happening right now, but which (in reality) isn't happening. In the example above, the implied meaning is

> If he were here, I would be so happy, but he isn't, so I am not.

It can be used also to express that something could theoretically happen in the future, but which we consider unlikely. For example,

> If she <u>came</u> tomorrow, I would take her to the park.

means

> It is possible (even though unlikely) that she will come tomorrow, and, if this is the case, I will take her to the park.

A few more examples to make the concept clearer:

> If John <u>knew</u> the answer, he would tell you. (correct)
>
> If John would know the answer, he would tell you. (correct)

If he <u>saw</u> what they are doing, he would call the police. (correct)

If he would see what they are doing, he would call the police. (wrong)

Notice there is no sequence of tenses in the last example. In an indicative sentence, we would say "He saw what they were doing" because "seeing" and "doing" happened at the same time. Here, however, the hypothetical situation is only "seeing"; "doing" does happen in reality, so there is no reason to use the subjunctive for it.

Speaking about the sequence of tenses... As I have already mentioned in the previous section, the subjunctive and the conditional don't change when used in reported speech (something that could hypothetically be happening continues to be hypothetical even when we speak about it later):

What Sheila said: *"If I had more money, I would buy a car."*

Sheila said that if she <u>had</u> more money, she would buy a car. (correct)

Sheila said that if she had had more money, she would have bought a car. (wrong)

"Would" can be used in this conditional form as the past subjunctive of "will" in the sense of "be willing to". For example, it can be used to make a polite request:

If you would pass me that bottle... Thanks.

Another common source of would's after if's is the phrase "would like". It is not only appropriate to use "would like" after "if" to make a polite suggestion; it would be wrong to make "would" disappear just because of 'if':

If you would like to listen to music, I could turn on the radio. (cor.)

If you liked to listen to music, I could turn on the radio. (wrong)

The latter example doesn't really make sense; the implied meaning would be "If you liked to listen to music, I could turn on the radio, but you don't like that, so I can't turn it on."

"If you would have done this, I would have done that."

Finally, if the hypothetical situation took place in the past and the result can no longer be modified, we use the format:

If X had happened, Y would have done Z.

The implied meaning is

If X had happened, Y would have done Z, but X didn't happen, so Y didn't do Z.

For example:

If he <u>had had</u> a bicycle, he <u>could have gone</u> on the biking trip with us.
If he would have had a bicycle, he could have gone on the biking trip with us. (wrong)

Again, "would" can be used as a verb implying some sort of willingness. Both

If Sandy <u>had learned</u> for her final exam, she would have got a better grade.

and

If Sandy would have learned for her final exam, she would have got a better grade.

are grammatically correct, but the form used in the first one is more common in practice. It means that Sandy didn't learn for her final, and, as a consequence, she got a bad grade; the other one says that had sandy been *willing to* learn for her final, she would have got better grades.

As a side note: The form I used in the last sentence is an alternative to "If ... had ...". For example:

"Had I known" = "If I had known"

Wish + would

The subjunctive mood is used to express something that (theoretically) could be happening right now, but which (in reality) isn't happening. And this is exactly what you need when you express a *wish*, for example:

> *I wish you were here. (correct)*
> *I wish you would be here. (wrong)*

Since it is the subjunctive, not the past tense, the correct formal form for I/he/she/it is also "were", not was. Note, however, that it is quite common to use "was" in informal speech by native speakers:

> *I wish she were here. (correct, formal)*
> *I wish she was here. (informal)*
> *I wish she would be here. (wrong)*

Even so, expressions of the form "I wish he would do something" are also *grammatically* correct but mean something else! As you have learned in the last section, "would" is the past subjunctive of the verb "will" in the sense of "be willing to".

In this sense, you can say that "you wish someone *would do* something" in order to express that "you wish someone were willing to do something". For example,

> *I wish you wouldn't smoke.*

expresses that you wish the other person were so kind as not to smoke. You find the fact that they smoke *unkind* or *irritating*. When you say

> *I wish you didn't smoke.*

you merely express that your conversational partner does smoke and that you wish otherwise, without the emotional subtext.

Note that, since the mood used after "wish" is the subjunctive, it doesn't change in reported speech:

> What Bob said: *"I wish I knew more about it."*
>
> *Bob said that he <u>wished</u> he <u>knew</u> more about it. (correct)*
> *Bob said that he wished he had known more about it. (wrong)*

COULD/COULDN'T CARE LESS

It's always been a mystery to me why some people say "I could care less". If you "could care less", you express indifference—you care somewhat, so you could care also less. You could perhaps care even more.

The point of the idiom is to express that you don't care. In fact, you care so little that you *couldn't care less*; you've already hit the bottom of how much care you give:

> *Oh, so he got arrested? I couldn't care less about him. (correct)*
> *Oh, so he got arrested? I could care less about him. (wrong)*

CONTINUE DOING/TO DO

Apparently, there is a belief among English teachers in China that "continue to do" and "continue doing" mean two different things. According to them, "continue to do" means "start doing something again that was previously interrupted", whereas "continue doing" means "to carry on the same thing you have already been doing".

Native speakers make no such conscious distinction. The one or the other form may sound better in certain situations or be more preferred in certain parts of the English speaking world, but this has more to do with the rhythm of the language rather than there being a strict dictionary definition separating the two. For example:

I will continue to improve my skills.
I will continue improving my skills.

mean completely the same. Some speakers may prefer the first variant, some the other one, but none of these will tell you whether you stopped improving your skills and started again before.

LEARNT OR LEARNED

Both "learned" and "learnt" are considered correct as the past tense and past participle of "learn". However, the spelling "learnt" is almost non-existent in modern American English.

There was almost no difference in popularity between the two forms in the UK until around 1940s, but "learned" is now the preferred form in the UK as well, so, especially if you are writing for an international audience, it's better to stick with "learned".

There is also a difference in pronunciation between the two forms: "learned" is pronounced /lɜːnd/ (UK) resp. /lɜːrnd/ (US), i.e. with a "D" at the end, whereas "learnt" is pronounced /lɜːnt/.

Note that "learned" is also an adjective (now relatively uncommon) meaning "having a lot of knowledge". Its pronunciation differs from the verb; in the UK, it is /ˈlɜːnɪd/, in the US, /ˈlɜːrnɪd/. To see how a word can fall out of fashion, take a look at the following diagram comparing the use of "learned" as a verb and as an adjective in English literature over the years (you will learn more about such diagrams in the last chapter of the book):

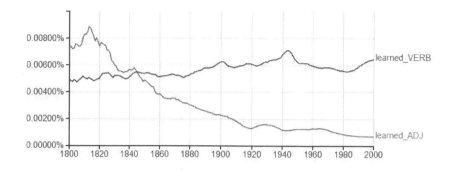

Effect or affect

Both "effect" and "affect" can be used as a noun or as a verb. The odds are that if you want to use a noun, you want to say "effect", as in

> *It has a negligible effect on me. (correct)*
> *It has a negligible affect on me. (wrong)*

and if you want to use a verb, you want to say "affect", as in

> *It affected me negatively. (correct)*
> *It effected me negatively. (wrong)*

"To effect" means "to implement (a policy)"; for example, one can "effect political changes". An "affect" (which is pronounced /ˈæfɛkt/) is a term used in psychology to mean a subjective feeling experienced in response to a stimulus. Both these terms are quite uncommon.

I CUT, YOU CUT, HE CUT

Most of the commonly used English verbs are irregular. If the past tense and the past participle differ from the present tense, it is usually not hard to remember these; for example, few learners would say "taked" instead of "took" and "taken". However, there is a certain class of verbs that commonly cause problems: verbs whose past tense is the same as the present tense.

Take, for example, the verb "cut". The past tense of "cut" is also "cut", so you could say both

> *I cut vegetables every day in the kitchen.*

and

> *I cut some paper yesterday.*

Usually, you would have to guess the meaning from the context, but if the verb is in the third person singular, you can tell by looking at its ending: "he cut" can only be in the past tense because the present tense would be "he cuts". For this reason, the entries in the following list are of the form "to **do** – he does – he did – he has done". The purpose of this section is to allow you to get used to the past tense of these verbs; just read the list and let your subconscious internalize the right form:

- to **bet** – he bets – he bet – he has bet
- to **broadcast** – he broadcasts – he broadcast – he has broadcast
- *Note: most dictionaries list also "broadcasted" as a possible form, but this form is not commonly used in practice.*
- to **burst** – he bursts – he burst – he has burst
- to **cut** – he cuts – he cut – he has cut
- to **cost** – it costs – it cost – it has cost
- to **cast** – he casts – he cast – he has cast

- to **fit** – it fits – it fit/ted – it has fit/ted

  In the US, the past tense and past participle are usually "fit", whereas in the UK they are usually "fitted". However, when used as adjectives, "fit" means healthy or appropriate, and fitted means designed to fit, both in the US and in the UK.

- to **forecast** – he forecasts – he forecast – he has forecast
- to **hit** – he hits – he hit – he has hit
- to **hurt** – it hurts – it hurt – it has hurt
- to **let** – he lets – he let – he has let
- to **miscast** – he miscasts – he miscast – he has miscast

  Note: "to miscast" means "to choose an unsuitable actor for a role".

- to **offset** – it offsets – it offset – it has offset

  Note: "to offset" means "to compensate" in relation to costs.

- to **put** – he puts – he put – he has put
- to **quit** – he quits – he quit – he has quit
- to **recast** – he recasts – he recast – he has recast
- to **reset** – he resets – he reset – he has reset
- to **retrofit** – he retrofits – he retrofit/ted – he has retrofit/ted

  Note: "to retrofit" means "to equip something with a part it didn't originally have". The same note as for "fit/ted" applies also here.

- to **set** – he sets – he set – he has set
- to **shed** – it sheds – it shed – it has shed
- to **shut** – he shuts – he shut – he has shut
- to **slit** – he slits – he slit – he has slit
- to **spit** – he spits – he spit/spat – he has spit/spat

  Note: the form "spit" is popular in the US; in the UK the past tense is "spat".

- to **sublet** – he sublets – he sublet – he has sublet
- to **spread** – he spreads – he spread – he has spread
- to **typecast** – he typecasts – he typecast – he has typecast

  Note: usually used in the passive. For an actor "to be typecast" means "to be always given the same type of character to play".

- to **typeset** – he typesets – he typeset – he has typeset
- to **undercut** – he undercuts – he undercut – he has undercut

  Note: "to undercut" means "to sell goods below your competitor's prices".

- to **upset** – it upsets – it upset – it has upset
- to **wed** – he weds – he wed/ded – he has wed/ded

  Note: "to wed" is an old-fashioned term for "to marry". Both "wed" and "wedded" are in use.

- to **wet** – he wets – he wet/ted – he has wet/ted

  Note: both "wet" and "wetted" are in use.

In addition to the verbs above, you should remember the verbs

- to **beat** – he beats [*beets*] – he beat [*beet*] – he has beaten
- to **read** – he reads [*reeds*] – he read [*red*] – he has read [*red*]

The past tense of "beat" is also "beat" (the past participle can be "beat" as well, but this form is often considered colloquial). The past tense and the past participle of "read" are also "read" but pronounced as "red".

WOULD OF

The expression "would of" is a common mistake. People who learn English mainly by ear (including many native speakers, unfortunately) sometimes try to write what they pronounce as "would *uhf*" and assume it must be "would of".

Grammatically, "of" doesn't make sense after "would". What they want to say is "would've", a contracted form of "would have". For example

I never would've thought that ... (correct, informal)
I never would have thought that ... (correct)
I never would of thought that ... (wrong)

Similarly, "could of" is a misspelling of "could've" and "should of" is a misspelling of "should've".

I ALREADY/NEVER/JUST HAVE DONE

When combining the present perfect ("have + past participle") and the words like "already", "never", "just", etc., they generally come after "have". A few examples:

She has only just arrived. (correct)
She only just has arrived. (wrong)

He has never been there. (correct)
He never has been there. (wrong)

They have already come. (correct)
They already have come. (wrong)

Note that "already" can also be moved to the end of the sentence for emphasis or to show irritation:

What do you want from me? I have done it already.

On the other hand, "yet" comes usually at the end of a sentence. Putting it right after "not" is possible, but it makes the sentence sound rather formal:

I haven't seen the document yet. (correct)
I have not yet seen the document. (correct, formal)

How/what does it look like

One thing I keep reading on the web is the expression "how does it look like?" Sadly, this sentence doesn't make sense. The correct way to express the thought is either "what does it look like?" or "how does it look?", for example:

> *I've heard he's got a new car. What does it look like? (correct)*
> *I've heard he's got a new car. How does it look? (correct)*
> *I've heard he's got a new car. How does it look like? (wrong)*

Although both questions are correct in this context, there's a slight difference in meaning. "How does it look?" is usually answered with a mere adjective:

> *Q: I've heard he's got a new car. How does it look?*
> *A: It looks good. / It's all right. / It's ugly.*

Of course, the thing you are asking about doesn't have to be "it", for example:

> *Q: You've got a new boyfriend? How does he look?*
> *A: I think he's cute.*

On the other hand, if you ask "what does he/she/it look like", you are inviting the other person to give you a more detailed description, usually using a comparison with a noun:

> *Q: You've got a new boyfriend? What does he look like?*
> *A: He looks like Johnny Depp.*

Nonetheless, the two sentences are interchangeable in most situations. Just remember not to use "look like" after "how".

How/what is it called

When you want to ask what the name of something is, the correct question is:

> *What is this thing called in English? (correct)*
> *How is this thing called in English? (wrong)*

Don't let your mother tongue mislead you; in most other languages, the translation would indeed use "how", not "what", but not in English.

If you want to use "how", you can try to form the question using the verb "say":

> *How do you say "Bratwurst" in English? (correct)*
> *What do you say "Bratwurst" in English? (wrong)*

There is one situation when "call" and "how" could be combined. You could ask a dog owner, "How do you call your dog?" However, the answer wouldn't be its name, as you might expect, but rather something like "Come here!" or "Using a whistle." The question would be synonymous to "In what way do you call your dog?"

Questions about the subject

Word order in questions in English is something people usually get used to very fast, but there is one case that commonly causes problems. If the interrogative pronoun is already the subject of the sentence, the word order is the same as in any ordinary sentence, e.g.

Who is she? (correct)
Who does she be? (wrong)

This causes little trouble for "who is" or "who are", but many people make a mistake when the pronoun is "what" or "which":

What killed him? (correct)
What did kill him? (wrong)

Which computer has a Blu-ray drive? (correct)
Which computer does have a Blu-ray drive? (wrong)

LOOK FORWARD TO HEAR(ING) FROM YOU

The "to" after "look forward" can be confusing because "to" is usually used to introduce a verb, as in "want to", "have to", etc. "To look forward to" uses a different pattern:

I look forward to [a thing you would like to happen].

Apparently, "hear" is not a thing, so it wouldn't make much sense to "look forward to hear from you". The thing you are looking forward to is "hearing from you":

I look forward to hearing from you. (correct)
I look forward to hear from you. (wrong)

As for the question whether to use "I look forward to" or "I am looking forward to", some people consider the two completely interchangeable, but most find the phrase with "look forward to" somewhat formal and best suited for formal correspondence, whereas "to be looking forward to" is more informal and friendly:

I look forward to hearing from you. (correct, formal)
I am looking forward to hearing from you. (correct, informal)

STAY OR STAND

To *stay* means "not to change location or value". "To stand" means "to be in a vertical position (on your feet)". For example:

I must stay at home today. (correct)
I must stand at home today. (wrong)

The latter sentence would imply that you can't sit down at home today (perhaps because there are no chairs there), but this is probably not what you want to say. If you want to express that you can't sit down, "stand" is appropriate:

I have to stand for 8 hours a day because I work manually. (correct)
I have to stay for 8 hours a day because I work manually. (wrong)

SO DON'T I/NEITHER DO I

Me *too* is an informal expression you would usually use to express that something applies to you *as well*, e.g.

A: I want to play a bit more.
B: Me too. [I also want to play a bit more.]

In a formal context (such as in an essay), we can use "so do I", "so am I", etc., for example:

He wants to go out. So do I.
She is angry. So am I.

So far, so good. However, the negation of "so do I" is not "so don't I", as some learners think, but rather "neither do I" or "nor do I":

He doesn't want to go out. Neither do I. (correct)
He doesn't want to go out. So don't I. (wrong)

She isn't angry. Nor am I. (correct)
She isn't angry. So aren't I. (wrong)

If you use the informal "me too", the negation is "me neither":

A: We don't want to play football.
B: Me neither. (correct) / Me too not. (wrong)

Put/take off one's hat

Whether you take off your hat literally or figuratively, the correct verb is "take":

He took off his hat when he came in. (correct)
He put off his hat when he came in. (wrong)

"Put off" doesn't really make sense here, as it means "to postpone" (you can say, for example, "she put off her homework to the last minute").

You can figuratively "take your hat off to someone" when you want to express respect or admiration, as in the following quotation by a British comedian:

Militant feminists, I take my hat off to them. They don't like that.

— Milton Jones

The reason why learners use "put off" is probably because the opposite action *is* expressed using "put":

> *When he left, he put his hat back on. (correct)*
> *When he left, he took his hat back on. (wrong)*

STAY/BE LEFT

Stay means "intentionally remain", so usually only a person can stay somewhere. You can say, for example:

> *I stayed at home.*
> *Lisa stayed at the airport.*

When you want to express the idea that a thing or a number of things remain somewhere, the expression you would usually choose is "to be left", as in

> *After he finished eating, there were only two yoghurts left in the fridge. (correct)*
> *After he finished eating, only two yoghurts stayed in the fridge. (wrong)*

The latter sentence would imply that the yoghurts were sentient beings, and only two of them decided to stay; the others left for a better life outside of the fridge.

Mistakes with adjectives, adverbs, and determiners

FAST, FASTLY, BUT NOT FURIOUSLY

Many English learners use the word "fastly" as an adverbial form of "fast", which seems quite logical because this is the way adverbs are usually formed. For example, if something is slow, you say that it "moves slowly", which is completely correct.

Unfortunately, languages develop in a way that is not always logical, and the situation of "fast" vs. "fastly" falls exactly into this category. The fact is that **there is no such word as "fastly"**. "Fast" is already both an adjective and an adverb, for example:

> *The athlete runs really fast. (correct)*
> *The athlete runs really fastly. (wrong)*

It doesn't matter whether "fast" refers to a movement or to the rate at which something is being done; it's always just "fast":

> *He can't write fast enough. (correct)*
> *He can't write fastly enough. (wrong)*

The word "quickly", used as an adverb, is synonymous to "fast", but it usually refers to the time an action takes rather than to the speed of movement. For example, when you say you want the other person to come *soon*; you don't really care how fast he or she will be moving. "Quickly" can also refer to the actual speed (as in "he runs quickly"), but such usage is much less common.

There is one situation in which it is obligatory to use "quickly" (or "swiftly" or a related adverb ending with "-ly") instead of "fast": if the adverb precedes the verb it modifies:

> *He quickly ran out of the building. (correct)*
> *He fast ran out of the building. (wrong)*
> *He fastly ran out of the building. (wrong)*

(A) LITTLE, (A) FEW

First, we will take a look at "a little" and "a few". Both mean essentially the same: "some", "a certain amount that is not large". "A little" is used with uncountable nouns (e.g. sugar), and "a few" is used with countable nouns (e.g. people), for example:

> *Could you please put a little sugar in my coffee? (correct)*
> *Could you please put a few sugar in my coffee? (wrong)*
>
> *I made a few friends in college. (correct)*
> *I made a little friends in college. (wrong)*

"A little" is more common than "a few" because it is used with abstract qualities, like knowledge or anger:

> *I know a little about the topic.*
> *She is a little upset.*

"Few" and "little" are used in the same vein—"few" with countable nouns and "little" with uncountable—but the meaning is different. They mean "almost no", "a negligible amount of", for example:

Few people would argue that it was a good decision. (correct)
Almost no people would argue that it was a good decision. (correct)
Little people would argue that it was a good decision. (wrong?)

I know little about the subject. (correct)
I know almost nothing about the subject. (correct)
I know few about the subject. (wrong)

The sentence starting with "Little people" above is grammatically correct, but it means that "small people would argue ...". "Little" and "few" can be used also in the sense of "not enough" which directly contrasts with "a little" and "a few". For example:

There is little milk left—could you buy some?
[There is not enough milk left—could you buy some?]

There is still a little milk; you don't have to buy any.
[There is still some milk; you don't have to buy any.]

SECOND OR OTHER

Imagine the following scenario: you are sitting next to a relative at a family gathering. There are two bottles that you cannot reach, and you would like to take one of them. You ask your neighbour: "Could you please pass me the bottle?" He can't see which of the two bottles you are pointing at, so he points at one of them and asks: "This one?" As it happens, it wasn't the correct one. How should you break this through to him?

In some languages, you'd literally say "No, the second one." In English, however, when there are only two options, we refer to the "second" option using the word "other", i.e. the correct way of saying that is:

> *A: Could you please pass me the bottle? [pointing at two bottles]*
> *B: This one?*
> *A: No, the other one. (correct) / A: No, the second one. (unnatural)*

Of course, this principle applies to every situation when you are referring to "the other" of two objects or people, for example:

> *Carlsen will probably beat the other player in tomorrow's chess match. (correct)*
> *Carlsen will probably beat the second player in tomorrow's chess match. (wrong)*

There are two players in a chess game. One of them plays as white, *the other one* plays as black, but there is no "first" or "second" player.

ALL THAT, ALL WHAT, ALL WHICH

What you most likely want to say is "all that ...", as in

> *All that glitters is not gold. (correct)*
> *All what glitters is not gold. (wrong)*
> *All which glitters is not gold. (wrong)*

The confusion stems from the fact that "all" is followed by "what" in many other languages, e.g. *alles was* in German. If you feel the need to say "all what" in English, the best option is usually to leave out the pronoun altogether:

This is all you need to know. (correct)
This is all what you need to know. (unnatural)

"All which" is not strictly speaking wrong, but it sounds rather formal and outdated (it was somewhat widespread before the 19th century).

BOTH AND EITHER

These two words tend to be translated using a single word into other languages. The meaning of "both" is usually quite clear. It means "the one as well as the other". When you speak about two restaurants, for instance, you can say:

Both restaurants are good.
[The one restaurant, as well as the other restaurant, is good.]

A common construction is "both X and Y ..." which means the same as "X and Y ..."; only the fact that the statement is true for X and Y *at the same time* is emphasized:

Both Peter and his father have red hair.
[Peter, as well as his father, has red hair.]

The situation is slightly complicated for "either" because it is used in two similar but different situations. "Either" can be used in the construction "either X or Y", which means "X or Y but not both". For example:

I'd like to eat either an apple or an orange.
[I'd like to eat an apple or an orange but not both of them at the same time.]

When "either" is not followed by "or", the logic stays the same. It means "any one of two possibilities but not both of them simultaneously". This is best illustrated by the most dangerous possible mis-understanding of the difference between "either" and "both": when it comes to dosing medication.

Suppose you tell your doctor you have two brands of painkillers at home, and you ask him or her which one of those you are supposed to take. If your doctor replies

> *"You can take either."*

it means you can take one or the other, but **not both of them simultaneously**, unless the doctor further clarifies that you can. If he or she, on the other hand, says

> *"You can take both."*

the implied meaning is that it is safe to take the one *and* the other at the same time.

FREEER OR FREER

Since the comparative form of short adjectives is formed by simply adding -er to the end of an adjective (apart from a few irregular adjectives like "good/better"), learners and native speakers alike sometimes think that when something is "more free", it should be "freeer".

The truth is that there is not a single word in English whose standard spelling would contain "eee". The simple rule is:

> *If you think there should be three e's in a row, write only two.*

For example, "most free" would be "freest", not "freeest". Note, however, that "freest" is pronounced as if it were written "freeest", i.e. /friːɪst/. The same goes for "freer", pronounced as /ˈfriːə(r)/.

"Free" is in fact the only comparable adjective ending in "ee", so there are no other such candidates for -eeer.

The -er suffix can be added also to verbs, where it expresses the person who does the action. For instance, someone who skies (/ski:z/, from the verb "to ski", not /skaɪz/, the plural of "sky") is a "skier", pronounced /ˈski:ə(r)/.

In the same vein, someone who sees (the future) is a "seer", not a "seeer", in accordance with the rule above. The pronunciation in this case is slightly more complicated. In British English, it is /si:ə/, i.e. exactly like "see" + "er". In American English, it can be either /si:ər/ or just /si:r/.

CLASSIC OR CLASSICAL

The word "classic" can be either an adjective or a noun. There's a beautiful and witty quote that explains the meaning of the noun:

'Classic' - a book which people praise and don't read.
— Mark Twain

A "classic" is a book, song, film, or any other piece of art that is considered to have set a high quality standard in its respective genre. Much less frequently, it is used also for the author of such a work.

Similarly, "a classic *thing*" is something that is in some way typical for its class, e.g. "a classic mistake":

This is a classic mistake English learners make. (correct)
This is a classical mistake English learners make. (probably wrong)

"Classical" means "traditional" or "being present for a long time". In science, for example, a "classical theory" is a theory that has well established itself as a useful scientific theory, although it often contrasts with another "modern theory" which is able explain more than the classical one. "Classical music" refers to well established music genres of the past centuries.

A classic example of the distinction between "classic" and "classical" is "a classic(al) example". A "classical example" means an example that has been around for a long time. But what you mean 99% of the time is "a classic example", which is the same as "a typical example".

"SYMPATHIC"

Sympathique in French, *sympathisch* in German, *sympatický* in Czech; the word has spread in some form probably to all European languages. With one major exception: English. That's right, "sympathic" is not an English word, as a quick search in any respectable dictionary will tell you.

So how do you translate "sympathic" (I'll use this word to refer to its meaning in other languages) into English when there is no such word? The fact is: you don't. There's no direct English equivalent for what "sympathic" is expected to mean by speakers of other languages, so you will have to work with words like "nice" and "kind":

> *She's a very nice girl. (correct)*
> *She's a sympathic girl. (wrong)*

You can also use the verb "like" if you find somebody "sympathic":

> *I like her. (correct)*
> *I find her sympathic. (wrong)*

There is one word that has a meaning similar to "sympathic": *congenial*. Unlike "sympathic" in other languages, "congenial" is a fairly formal word, and using it in an everyday conversation could make you sound pretentious, so I advise against using it unless you know what you are doing.

So far, so good, but there is one more trap many learners fall into. In English, there is a word "sympathetic", which means "compassionate to someone" or "approving of something", but <u>not</u> "sympathic":

> *She was a very sympathetic listener when I felt sad. (correct)*
> *I find her sympathic; she is nice and pretty. (wrong)*

MANY/SOME/FEW (OF)

Many, some, and similar expressions mean essentially the same whether you use them with or without "of", but the two variants are are not interchangeable. Before nouns without determiners ("the", "his", etc.), we don't use "of":

> *Many students study to get a better-paying job. (correct)*
> *Many of students study to get a better-paying job. (wrong)*
>
> *Some people can never be satisfied. (correct)*
> *Some of people can never be satisfied. (wrong)*

If there is a determiner (e.g. "the", "his") before the noun, we do use "of":

> *Some of the students failed the exam. (correct)*
> *Some the students failed the exam. (wrong)*
>
> *A few of my friends moved overseas. (correct)*
> *A few my friends moved overseas. (wrong)*

Before pronouns, we use "of" as well:

> *I've seen a few of them. (correct)*
> *I've seen a few them. (wrong)*

The word "both" seems to be a special case. Just like with the rest, we wouldn't use "of" with a bare noun, for example:

> *Both policemen were very friendly. (correct)*
> *Both of policemen were very friendly. (wrong)*

and we do use "of" before pronouns:

> *They want both of us to work for them. (correct)*
> *They want us both to work for them. (correct)*
> *They want both us to work for them. (wrong)*

Note that "us both" is more common than "both of us", but both expressions are correct.

It is not that common to use "both of" in connection with "the"; it is usually more elegant to reformulate the sentence with "both" in another position.

> *Both of the fastest sprinters share the same time. (possible)*
> *The fastest sprinters both share the same time. (better)*

However, there is a big difference when it comes to possessive pronouns. The variant without "of" is actually the preferred one:

> *Both my parents are doctors. (preferred)*
> *Both of my parents are doctors. (possible in American English)*

It is worth noting that "both of my/his/our/..." is virtually non-existent in British English, and it is more common even in American English as well. It is therefore better not to use "of" in this case.

Finally, there is an idiomatic expression with "many" which doesn't follow any of the patterns mentioned above, namely "many a". We can use "many a + singular noun" in the same sense as "many + plural noun", for example:

Many a learner doesn't know that "many" can be followed by "a".

This usage is limited mostly to formal writing, however, and is only rarely heard in the spoken language.

So/as fast as

When we compare two things which are similar or equal in some respect, we use the construction "as ... as ...", not "so ... as ...":

She is as fast/good/tall as him. (correct)
She is so fast/good/tall as him. (wrong)

When negating the sentence, using "not so ... as ..." was quite common historically, but it is slowly falling out of use. "Not as ... as ..." is much more common, so it is better for a learner to stick to "as ... as ..." in both cases, for example:

The film was not as good as the book. (correct)
The film was not so good as the book. (dated)

Like more/better/most/best

Both "like more" and "like better" (as in the sentence "I like apples more/better than oranges") are widespread, but "like more" is preferred in British English whereas Americans are more likely to choose "like better":

I like apples more than oranges. (correct)

I like apples better than oranges. (correct, colloquial in the UK)

Expressions "to like most" and "to like best" seem to be used interchangeably both in American and British English. Some speakers use the variant with "the", i.e. "to like the most/best", but others consider it less grammatical. It is therefore advisable to stick to the variant without "the":

I like him best. (correct)

I like him most. (correct)

I like him the most. (considered less grammatical by some)

I like him the best. (considered less grammatical by some)

LOOK/SMELL/FEEL GOOD/WELL

Sentences with the verb "look" (in the sense of "appear, seem") have a structure different from what many English learners think. "Look" is followed by an adjective, not an adverb:

He looks good. (correct)

He looks well. (see below)

Both sentences are grammatically correct, but "well" here was used as an adjective meaning "in good health", so:

"He looks good." = "He is good-looking."

"He looks well." = "He seems to be in good health."

It is **not** possible to say "he looks well" to express the idea that someone is handsome. For some reason, the difference between "good" and "well" is the most common source of mistakes; in other cases, learners usually use the adjective correctly:

She looks pretty. (correct)

She looks prettily. (wrong)

It looks large. (correct)

It looks largely. (wrong)

If you use "look" in the sense of seeing or searching, then "look well" where "well" is an adverb makes sense. For example, we could say:

If you look well, you will see it.

Such a construction is possible, but "carefully" is more common in this context:

If you look carefully, you will see it.

Smell and feel

The verbs "smell" and "feel" follow the exact same pattern as "look". If you like the smell of something, it smells "good", not "well":

The flower smells good. (correct)

The flower smells well. (wrong)

Unlike "look", something can't really "smell well"; we don't usually say that a thing or a person "smells healthy". An example for "feel":

I feel great. (correct)

I feel greatly. (wrong)

In the case of the verb "feel", it makes sense to "feel well" in the sense of feeling healthy:

"I feel good." = "I feel satisfied. I experience pleasant feelings."
"I feel well." = "I feel healthy. I feel physically fit."

A LOT OF/MUCH/LONG TIME AGO

The common way to say that "it's been a while since something happened" in English is "a long time ago", not "a lot of time ago" or "much time ago", e.g.

> *It was a long time ago when I first saw the sea. (correct)*
> *It was a lot of time ago when I first saw the sea. (wrong)*
> *It was much time ago when I first saw the sea. (wrong)*

This expression is also a nice example of how using search engines to judge grammaticality can be dangerous. By the time I was writing this book, Google returned "About 31,400,000 results" for "a lot of time ago". Can you guess how many times this expression was used in English literary works during the last 200 years? Not a single time.

MORE BETTER

The comparative degree ("more of something") of monosyllabic adjectives is usually formed by adding *-er* at the end of the adjective (such as "tall" and "taller"). Longer adjectives are usually compared using "more" (e.g. "expensive" and "more expensive"). This causes some learners to combine the two constructions and say "more better", "more taller", "more richer", etc.

Such usage is wrong. When something is "better", it is always just "better" and never "more better":

> *My car is better than yours. (correct)*
> *My car is more better than yours. (wrong)*

It would make sense, syntactically, to say that if "A and B are better than C", and "A is better than B", then "A is more better than C than B". Nevertheless, such construction is <u>not</u> used in practice, and you should use "even better", e.g.

B is better than C, and A is even better then B.

This doesn't necessarily mean that "better" cannot follow "more" in a sentence, for example:

We need more better people.

The structure of this sentence is "we need more X" where X can be anything, such as roses or better people.

YET OR ALREADY

The rule is simple for indicative sentences. "Already" is used in affirmative sentences, "yet" in negative ones (usually with the present perfect):

I have already finished my homework. (correct)
I have yet finished my homework. (wrong)

I haven't seen her yet. (correct)
I haven't seen her already. (wrong)

The situation changes when we want to ask a question. Both "yet" and "already" may be used in both affirmative and negative questions, and while "yet" is completely neutral, "already" implies some sort of surprise or unexpectedness. "Yet" would be probably the more common choice:

Have you finished your homework yet?
Haven't you spoken to him yet?

To illustrate the kind of situation in which "already" would be used, we'll take a look at two dialogues:

A: Thanks for the sandwich. It was really delicious.
B: Have you eaten it already? I gave it to you twenty seconds ago.

"Yet" would be inappropriate here; only "already" can express that B is surprised that A ate the sandwich so fast. Similarly, in a negative question:

A: Sorry, I must go. I have a lot of homework to do.
B: Haven't you already done your homework? You told me you did.

Again, "already" implies some kind of surprise.

Mistakes with prepositions

Get off, get out of, take off, exit

One of the most common activities and still causing trouble; do we *get off, get out of, take off,* or *exit* buses, trains, planes, and cars? The answer is: It depends on the vehicle. First of all, the verb "exit" can be used with any conceivable vehicle or building, but it sounds very formal. Consider the following sentence:

> *Terminal station. Please exit the train. (a formal announcement used in the Prague metro)*

"Exit" was appropriate here, as the whole expression was supposed to be understood as a formal command. On the other hand, it is too formal for a normal conversation:

> *I must exit the bus at the next stop. (too formal for a normal conversation)*

In normal speech, the preferred expression for a bus, train, plane, and other public transport vehicles would be to "get off". Although you can say that you "take a bus" when you "get <u>on</u> the bus" (not "in"), you can't say that you "take off the bus" when you "get off":

> *I must get off (the bus) at the next stop. (correct)*
> *I must take off (the bus) at the next stop. (wrong)*

The difference between "get off" and "get out of" is a little bit more delicate. We get *off* public transport, but we get *out of* a (personal) car, and never the other way round:

> *Get off the bus at the next stop. (correct)*
> *Get out of the bus at the next stop. (wrong)*
>
> *Get out of the car after you arrive. (correct)*
> *Get off the car after you arrive. (wrong)*

For the sake of completeness, we should mention that "get out of the bus" could be used in case of emergency as a command. A driver who noticed the bus was on fire could shout, "Everybody get out of the bus!" Nevertheless, this is hopefully not something you will ever need to say.

ARRIVE AT/IN/TO

Because of the influence of verbs like "come to", "move to", and "go to", learners of English often tend to use the combination "arrive" + "to". Although sentences such as "come to me", "we moved to London", or "are you going to the party?" are completely appropriate, "arrive" behaves somewhat differently.

There is only one context in which "arrive to" is appropriate, namely when "to" means "in order to", for example:

> *The cleaner arrived [in order] to clean the office.*

When you want to express that you come to a country, city, or generally a geographical location, use "arrive in". For example:

> *We will arrive in England at about 5 o'clock. (correct)*
> *We will arrive to England at about 5 o'clock. (wrong)*

Once you arrive in Paris, make sure to visit the Eiffel Tower. (cor.)
Once you arrive to Paris, make sure to visit the Eiffel Tower. (wr.)

In virtually any other situation, you should use "arrive at":

When I arrived at the party, all my friends were already drunk. (cor.)
When I arrived to the party, all my friends were already drunk. (wr.)

Please, arrive on time at the meeting point. (correct)
Please, arrive on time to the meeting point. (wrong)

Although some people would argue that the last sentence is an example of "arrive on", it is not so; "on time" should be treated as an idiomatic expression in its own right.

To be good at/in

When you want to express that you are well capable of doing something, the usual collocation is "to be good *at* something", e.g.

He is good at playing the piano. (correct)
He is good in playing the piano. (wrong)

Some native speakers do use "to be good in" when they talk about classes at school, e.g. "he is good in science" in the meaning of "he performs well in his science class". Others, however, consider such an expression unnatural, so you may want to avoid it altogether.

There are some idiomatic expressions where "good in" is appropriate, but these are rather rare. The most common one is "to be good in bed", meaning "to perform well in sex":

She is good in bed. (correct)
She is good at bed. (wrong)

Obviously, one cannot be good *at* bed, since "bed" is not an activity.

DIFFERENT FROM/THAN/TO

Is the meaning of "different from" different to "different than" and that of "different than" different from "different to"? I was just jok-ing, but hopefully I've got my message across, namely that there's no difference in meaning among the three expressions.

The only difference is that of commonness. "Different from" (as in "A is different from B") is the most common one. "Different than" is used mostly in the United States and not so much in the UK, whereas "different to" is common in British English but uncommon in Amer-ican English. Nevertheless, neither of them is considered incorrect on either side of the Atlantic, and you will be understood if you use any of the three.

ON/IN THE PHOTO

The equivalent expression in many languages would use a preposi-tion translated usually as "on" (e.g. *sur* in French). In English, how-ever, the correct preposition is "in":

> *The boy in the photo looks sad. (correct)*
> *The boy on the photo looks sad. (wrong)*

The pattern is the same no matter what word we use for the visual media (e.g. image, photo, picture, drawing):

> *There are no trees in the picture. (correct)*
> *There are no trees on the picture. (wrong)*

We only use "on" when we mean that something is on top of a physical object. For example "there's a cup on a photo" means that the cup lies on a photo. "On" can also be used when one thing is part of the top layer of another thing. This can be a little confusing for words like "postcard". We would say:

> *There's a [picture of a] house on a postcard. (correct)*
> *There's a [picture of a] house in a postcard. (wrong)*

The reason is that a postcard is the piece of paper itself, not what's printed on it (unlike the word "picture", which refers to the actual visual content). Similarly, if you saw a picture of a man drawn on an envelope, you wouldn't say that there's a man *in* the envelope, would you. The (picture of the) man is *on* the envelope.

SUITED FOR/TO

It's hard to make a mistake in this case, as both "suited for" and "suited to" are correct, and the same applies to "ill-suited" and "well-suited"). Some native speakers feel there is a subtle difference in meaning, but for most the expressions are equivalent:

> *She is well suited for the job. (correct)*
> *She is well suited to the job. (correct)*

As for the hyphen, "well-suited" and "ill-suited" are used when they modify nouns, "well suited" and "ill suited" when "something is well/ill suited", for example:

> *It's such a well-suited car. (correct)*
> *It's such a well suited car. (wrong)*

It is also quite widespread to say "well-suited to do something", but it is usually more elegant to just omit verb:

> *This computer is well suited to the task. (correct)*
> *This computer is well suited to do the task. (less elegant)*

MARRIED TO/WITH

When you say that someone is or gets married, and you want to specify the person whom he or she marries, the correct preposition is "to", not "with", e.g.

> *Peter is married to Jane. (correct)*
> *Peter is married with Jane. (wrong)*

The same goes for "marriage with/to". Although "marriage with" is sometimes used, especially when referring to historical marriages, such as that of a king or a queen, "marriage to" is much more common:

> *Her marriage to Peter wasn't the happiest. (correct)*
> *Her marriage with Peter wasn't the happiest. (unnatural)*

TIME PREPOSITIONS

The rules for time prepositions are relatively simple. We use "at" for a particular **time of day**:

- *at 5 o'clock*
- *at 9:37 am*
- *at noon*

- *at night*

We use "on" (not "at") for a **particular day**:

- *on Tuesday*
- *on 17 June 2014 (on the seventeenth of June 2014)*
- *on Christmas Day*
- *on her birthday*

And, finally, we use "in" for months and longer periods (seasons, years, centuries, etc.):

- *in August*
- *in the winter*
- *in 1999*
- *in the last century*

There are a few expressions that don't fit the scheme above. For **holidays lasting more than a day**, we usually use "at":

- *at Christmas*
- *at Easter*

"**Morning**", "**afternoon**", and "**evening**" are preceded with "in the" when they mean a particular time of day:

  I usually drink tea in the morning/afternoon/evening.

When "in" or "at" clashes with "on" used for days, "on" wins:

- *on Monday morning*
- *on Wednesday afternoon*
- *on Friday evening*
- *on Sunday night*

Finally, when speaking about the **weekend**, the British use "at", and Americans use "on":

- *at the weekend [British English]*
- *on the weekend [American English]*

CALL (TO) SOMEONE

When you make a phone call, you *call someone*. There is no "to" in the English expression:

> *I have to call my mother to ask her something. (correct)*
> *I have to call to my mother to ask her something. (wrong)*

Perhaps you know the song *Call Me Maybe* (written and sung by Carly Rae Jepsen), which should help you remember to leave out the "to":

> *[...] but here's my number, so call me maybe. (correct)*
> *[...] but here's my number, so call to me maybe. (wrong)*

I'VE BEEN HERE FOR/SINCE/DURING TIME

For is used with an amount of time, and it expresses *how long* you have been doing something. "Since" is used with a date (or a time of day), and it expresses the date (or time) when you *started* doing something. For example, you can say:

> *I've been doing my homework for three hours. (correct)*
> *I've been doing my homework since three hours. (wrong)*

You must use "for" here because "three hours" is the *amount* of time you have spent doing your homework. On the other hand, in

> *I've been doing my homework since yesterday. (correct)*
> *I've been doing my homework for yesterday. (wrong)*

you can only use "since" because you express *when* you started doing your homework (yesterday), not how long you've been doing it.

Finally, some learners try to use "during" in such sentences instead of "for", but such usage is not correct:

I've been doing my homework for three hours. (correct)

I've been doing my homework during three hours. (wrong)

Mistakes with commas

No discussion about the most common mistakes in English would be complete without mentioning commas. Although not using commas properly would not make you *sound* unnatural (as it is a purely typographical device), it would make your writing look substandard or even cause misunderstanding.

COMMA BEFORE A DEPENDENT CLAUSE

What sets English apart from most other languages is its use of comma before a dependent (subordinate) clause. Dependent clauses (clauses introduced by words like "that", "which", "who", "where", "how", etc.) are **neither preceded nor followed by a comma**. For example:

> *Cars that don't have seat belts aren't allowed to carry children. (cor.)*
> *Cars, that don't have seat belts, aren't allowed to carry children. (w.)*

> *I don't know which one I want. (correct)*
> *I don't know, which one I want. (wrong)*

> *Could you tell me where it is? (correct)*
> *Could you tell me, where it is? (wrong)*

Dependent clauses are separated with commas only when the information contained in the clause is not important for the overall meaning of the whole sentence. A good way to recognize such clauses is to try to enclose the clause in parentheses; if the sentence still makes sense, you should use commas (or parentheses) to separate the clause from the rest, e.g.

> *Brazil nuts, which you can buy in a supermarket,*
> *are a great source of selenium.*

Commas were appropriate here because we could replace them with parentheses:

> *Brazil nuts (which you can buy in a supermarket) are a great source*
> *of selenium.*

Not using commas or parentheses would be a mistake in this case. The sentence

> *Brazil nuts which you can buy in a supermarket are a great source of*
> *selenium.*

implies that only Brazil nuts sold in a supermarket are a great source of selenium, which is certainly not the case.

Notice how the three examples we used at the beginning wouldn't make sense if we put the dependent clause in parentheses:

> *Cars (that don't have seat belts) aren't allowed to carry children.*
> *I don't know (which one I want).*
> *Could you tell me (where it is)?*

COMMA BEFORE CONJUNCTIONS BETWEEN INDEPENDENT CLAUSES

Most languages don't require a comma before "and" when it joins two independent clauses, but writing a comma before "but", "so", and other conjunctions is quite common. In English, however, we don't make a difference between "and" and other conjunctions, and you should almost always use a comma:

> *I had to go to the airport, and/but/so I couldn't attend the party. (co.)*
> *I had to go to the airport and/but/so I couldn't attend the party. (wr.)*

> *She's already seen the film, and she doesn't want to go. (correct)*
> *She's already seen the film and she doesn't want to go. (wrong)*

I wrote "almost always" because it is usually considered acceptable to omit the comma when both clauses are very short, e.g.

> *I played the guitar and she sang. (acceptable)*
> *I played the guitar, and she sang. (correct)*

The solution seems to be simple: just write the comma every time, and you cannot be wrong. But, there is a catch. When "and", "but", and other conjunctions separate just two verbs, not two clauses, we don't use a comma, for example:

> *He cooks and eats. (correct)*
> *He cooks, and eats. (wrong)*

> *He can ride a bike but can't swim. (correct)*
> *He can ride a bike, but can't swim. (wrong)*

The problem is that you can make the sentence any length you wish; as long as there is no subject in the other "clause", you shouldn't use a comma:

> *He cooks meals for the whole family and eats a lot of vegetables. (cor.)*
> *He cooks meals for the whole family, and eats a lot of vegetables. (wr.)*

Theoretically, you could avoid this situation by always putting the subject in each part of the sentence, but this can hardly be recommended; you will certainly agree the following sentence sounds a bit clumsy:

He cooks meals for the whole family, and he eats a lot of vegetables.

The sentence is grammatically correct, but the one without "he" and the comma sounds much more natural.

COMMA BETWEEN INDEPENDENT CLAUSES

It is perfectly fine to separate two sentences by a comma in most European languages. In English, however, this is considered a mistake; you either have to use a full stop (period), a semicolon (like I did in this sentence), or you have to use a conjunction (a word like "and", "but", "whereas", etc.):

Jane went to the cinema. John went home. (correct)
Jane went to the cinema; John went home. (correct)
Jane went to the cinema, and John went home. (correct)
Jane went to the cinema, John went home. (wrong)

We use a semicolon especially when there is some logical connection between the two clauses (i.e. when we don't use a conjunction, but the sentence doesn't look quite right with a full stop), for example:

I moved to Japan; I want to stay there. (correct)
I moved to Japan, and I want to stay there. (correct)
I moved to Japan. I want to stay there. (somewhat fragmented)
I moved to Japan, I want to stay there. (wrong)

The third example is grammatically correct, but the style is somewhat inappropriate. Too many short sentences may make your writing look childish or non-native.

Moreover, if the latter clause/sentence is introduced by an adverb like "moreover", "nevertheless", "however", etc., you should use a full stop or a semicolon:

I moved to Japan. Moreover, I intend to stay there. (correct)

I moved to Japan, moreover, I intend to stay there. (wrong)

Jane went to the cinema; however, John went home. (correct)

Jane went to the cinema, however, John went home. (wrong)

Don't confuse this usage with such adverbs modifying the *first* clause, as in:

I was originally thinking about moving to China. I moved to Japan, however, and I intend to stay there.

"However" belongs to the first clause, not to the second; we could as well have said "However, I moved to Japan, and I intend to stay there."

COMMA AFTER INTRODUCTORY PHRASE

After an introductory phrase, you should usually write a comma. I intentionally started the last sentence with an introductory phrase to demonstrate what an introductory phrase is: it is a part of sentence that would normally come after a verb (without any comma). If you break the natural flow, you should indicate it with a comma:

After an introductory phrase, you should write a comma. (correct)
You should write a comma after an introductory phrase. (correct)
After an introductory phrase you should write a comma. (wrong)

Before moving any further, let us introduce a few concepts. (correct)
Before moving any further let us introduce a few concepts. (wrong)

If you feel the flow of the sentence would be harmed by including a comma (which indicates a short pause), you may omit it. Such usage should be limited to short adverbial phrases indicating time, place, or manner, for example:

> *Yesterday I saw him.*
> *With gratitude he accepted the prize.*

Nonetheless, writing a comma in these sentences would be also considered completely correct.

Whether you use a comma or not, *don't overuse introductory phrases*. I've seen many texts (especially in scientific writing) written by non-native speakers in which almost every other sentence started with an introductory phrase. It is fine to use an introductory phrase every now and then to emphasize a certain part of the sentence, but this is not the normal way to construct sentences are in English. "I saw him yesterday." is the normal way. "Yesterday(,) I saw him." makes the sentence sound more dramatic and puts more emphasis on "yesterday".

There is one type of short introductory phrases which should always be followed by a comma. Adverbs like "however", "nevertheless", "moreover", "therefore", etc., are always followed by a comma when used at the beginning of a sentence to provide a logical connection with what was said previously, for example:

> *I like him. However, I wouldn't want to work with him. (correct)*
> *I like him. However I wouldn't want to work with him. (wrong)*

> *I cleaned the bathroom. Moreover, I took out the rubbish. (correct)*
> *I cleaned the bathroom. Moreover I took out the rubbish. (wrong)*

(Note that "rubbish" is a British expression for what would be usually called "trash" or "garbage" in American English.) The comma is especially important in the case of "however" because without a comma, it means "no matter how", for example:

> *However much you try, you cannot win. (correct)*
> *However, much you try, you cannot win. (wrong)*

COMMA AND 'IF'

The conjunction "if" behaves just like "which", "where", "who", etc.; that is, if it introduces a clause important for the overall meaning of the sentence, we don't use a comma before it (both in the meaning of "whether" and in the meaning of "when"):

> *I don't know if he comes. (correct)*
> *I don't know, if he comes. (wrong)*

> *Please let me know if something happens. (correct)*
> *Please let me know, if something happens. (wrong)*

Just like with the other conjunctions, only use a comma as an alternative to parentheses. There is, however, one important difference in usage. Unlike "which", "where", etc., "if" is often used at the beginning of a sentence (as a sort of an introductory phrase), and such a clause is always followed by a comma:

> *If the Potters come, there won't be enough chairs for all. (correct)*
> *If the Potters come there won't be enough chairs for all. (wrong)*

> *If something happens, please let me know. (correct)*
> *If something happens please let me know. (wrong)*

"Which", "where", and other conjunctions can also be used in this way, but such style is considered very formal and literary, and would be found mostly in older literature, poetry, and similar works of art:

> *What he told him, I don't know. (correct, literary)*

This construction should be avoided in normal writing and speech.

Comma before 'because'

Because introduces a dependent clause that almost always contains essential information, so just like before "that", "which", "who", etc., we usually don't use a comma, e.g.

> *I must go to work now because my boss told me so. (correct)*
> *I must go to work now, because my boss told me so. (see below)*

The latter example implies that the fact that your boss told you so is mostly irrelevant—but why mention it then? A good rule of thumb is: If you don't feel the need to put the clause starting with "because" in parentheses, don't use a comma.

There is one important class of exceptions, however. When the first clause is negative, not affirmative, it is often recommended to use a comma to avoid possible misreading. The Chicago Manual of Style gives the following example:

> *He didn't run, because he was afraid.*

This sentence can only be interpreted as "He didn't run, and the reason was that he was afraid." If we don't use a comma, it can be misunderstood as "The reason why he didn't run wasn't that he was afraid.", as in:

> *He didn't run because he was afraid. He ran because he enjoys running.*

If the meaning is clear even without a comma, you can omit it, but you should use a comma whenever the first reading can result in misunderstanding.

Note that if the order of the *because*-clause and the main clause is reversed, we always use a comma, just like for "if":

Because he was afraid, he didn't run. (correct)
Because he was afraid he didn't run. (wrong)

SERIAL (OXFORD) COMMA

As you might have noticed, when there is a list of the form "A, B, ...,
X, and Y" in this book, there is always a comma before "and". This is
not a matter of correctness; if I omitted the commas, no-one could
say that I made a mistake. However, the style I use is so common you
should learn how it is used.

What I use is the so called *serial comma* or *Oxford comma* (or *Harvard
comma*). For instance, in this book I wrote:

> *Just like water, sugar, and love, money can be used ... (ser. comma)*

Without the Oxford comma, the sentence would read:

> *Just like water, sugar and love, money can be used ... (no ser. comma)*

My personal feeling is that the Oxford comma improves clarity most
of the time; for example, "water, sugar and love, money" in the sentence above without the comma may seem to be the first three items
in a list that goes on, whereas "water, sugar, and love" makes it un-
ambiguously clear that the list ended there. A famous example is a
book dedication of the form:

> *To my parents, Ayn Rand, and God.*

The meaning is completely clear. Without the comma:

> *To my parents, Ayn Rand and God.*

Is the author claiming that he or she is the child of Ayn Rand and
God? Probably not, but this is not clear from the punctuation.

The Oxford comma can, in much rarer cases, also create ambiguity. Imagine a dedication like:

> *To my mother, Ayn Rand, and God.*

Is Ayn Rand the mother's name, or are the mother and Ayn Rand two different people? Nevertheless, such ambiguities can virtually always be resolved using different punctuation marks or word order, e.g.

> *To my mother (Ayn Rand) and God.*
> *To my mother, God, and Ayn Rand.*

Ambiguities created by not using the serial comma are often much harder (or even impossible) to resolve.

COMMA AROUND 'ETC.'

Should you use a comma before and after "etc."? There's no definitive answer, because different style guides recommend different usage. Nevertheless, the style that seems to be recommended most of the time is to *always include a comma before "etc."*; it is recommended even by those who discourage the use of the Oxford comma. For example:

> *He bought some apples, oranges, grapefruits, etc.*

If "etc." is not the last part of the sentence, it is also to be **followed** by a comma:

> *He bought some apples, oranges, grapefruits, etc., for his fruit salad.*

Some sources recommend not using any comma at all, e.g.

> *He bought some apples, oranges, grapefruits etc. for his fruit salad.*

but these are quite uncommon, and such usage is usually perceived negatively by those who do use the comma.

Online tools

This book taught you some of the most common mistakes English learners make, but no book can teach you everything. To be able to learn on your own and to make your speech and writing sound natural, you will need a tool which will allow you to judge whether a phrase you are about to use is grammatical.

There is a good tool and a bad tool for that, made by the same company. Unfortunately, most English learners don't know the good tool and use the bad tool, and that is why I would like to pinpoint the important qualities of the good tool and the drawbacks of the bad tool.

Avoid Google search to judge grammar

Most people check grammar online by performing a Google search on several variants of the expression they are not sure about and use the one with the greatest number of results. This approach is flawed for several reasons:

1. There are about 1.5 billion people with some knowledge of English in the world, but only about 400 million of these are native speakers. In other words, there are a huge number of people using English on the Internet who are likely to make the same mistake you are trying to avoid.

2. Google *estimates* the number of results using complicated algorithms because it is technically *impossible* to count the real number of occurrences of a term in all pages on the Internet. The number can be quite accurate for one term while it may be completely off for another.

3. There are some differences between British and American English (and other English varieties) and also between formal and informal language. Google Search will only tell you

whether some English speakers somewhere use the expression, but not whether it is suitable for your intended audience.

The Ngram viewer

Now to the good tool: The **Google Ngram Viewer** is a tool which allows you to overcome all of the problems mentioned above, and it is available for free at books.google.com/ngrams/. When you open the page, you will see something similar to the following picture:

Google has a huge database of digitized books. When you type a word or a phrase in the Ngram viewer, it will show you how common the phrase was throughout the years compared to all phrases that have the same number of words. For example, the picture shows us that if we randomly select two subsequent words from all English books available in the corpus published in the year 2000, we will get "Albert Einstein" with probability of approximately 0.0001%.

The number itself is not very interesting, but the relative frequency of a phrase compared to another one is. When you type several phrases separated by commas, the Ngram viewer will plot the curves for all the terms in one picture (as you can see above). This is a great tool to judge which variant of a phrase sounds more natural. Say, you are unsure about the distinction between "I did it yesterday" and "I have done it yesterday", so you type both phrases in the Ngram viewer. You will get the following result:

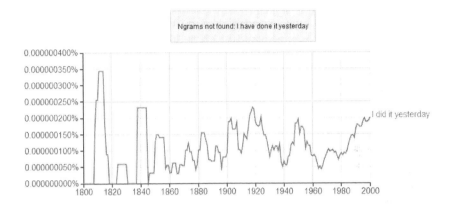

The phrase "I have done it yesterday" wasn't found a single time in the corpus while "I did it yesterday" seems to be moderately popular. This indicates there's clearly something wrong with the former (and that you should probably avoid it).

There are two options you should care about: *case sensitivity* and *corpus*. By default, the *case-insensitive* checkbox is left unchecked, and the system will try to find the phrase exactly as you wrote it, e.g. the query "he did" will not match "He did". It is usually better to check the checkbox, but if you want to check whether a phrase may be used at the beginning of a sentence, you may leave it unchecked and start your phrase with a capital letter.

The *corpus* option is important if you want to distinguish American and British usage. By selecting "American English" or "British English" from the list, you can check how common a phrase is just in American and British literature, respectively.

The last thing I would like to mention about the Ngram viewer is its ability to distinguish which part of speech every word represents. From time to time, you will find a phrase which is ambiguous because some of the words can be interpreted in several ways. For example, imagine you are not sure about the past participle of the verb "water" (as in "to water plants"), and you want to check the variants "has water" and "has watered", which yields:

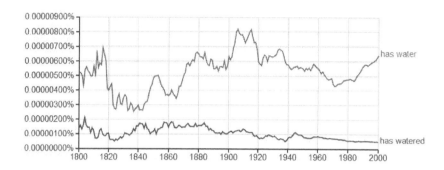

Does it mean that "has water" is more common as the present perfect of "to water"? Of course not! The phrase "has water" is so common because it makes perfect sense to "have water" in the sense of having the liquid. To avoid that, you can add various "suffixes" to the words in your query to specify the part of speech, e.g. _VERB, _NOUN, _ADJ, _ADV, and others (the full list can be found at books.google.-com/ngrams/info). When we add _VERB to our watery example, we get the expected result:

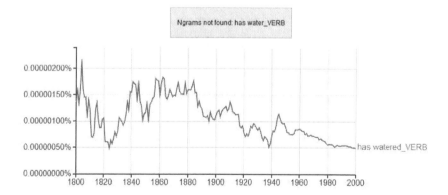

Final remarks

Thank you for reading this book; I hope you enjoyed the process of learning about the most common mistakes in English. If you liked the book, you could be interested in my book about the most common **pronunciation mistakes** (entitled *Improve your English pronunciation and learn over 500 commonly mispronounced words*):

http://jakubmarian.com/pronunciation/

Several other books on issues English learners must face are currently under preparation, and a lot of freely available information can be found at

www.jakubmarian.com

You can also follow me on:

Facebook: http://www.facebook.com/JakubMarianOfficial

Google+: http://gplus.to/JakubMarian

Mailing list: http://jakubmarian.com/mailing-list/

Should you find any mistake in the book (apart from the intentionally included ones), please, send me an email to

errors@jakubmarian.com

Alphabetical Index

Made in the USA
Lexington, KY
07 August 2016